IN DEDICATION

*To my mother and father who have
been a major part of my life
and to my partners,
Mico, Bob, Dick and Ray who
have made all of this possible.*

Restaurant Reinvention Press
2711 Cedar Springs Road
Dallas, Texas 75201

Designed by SmithMay, Dallas, Texas

Manufactured in the United States of America

ISBN 0-9716576-0-2

RESTAURANT LIFE

THE CULINARY CHRONICLES OF CHEF CHRIS WARD

RESTAURANT REINVENTION PRESS

TABLE OF CONTENTS

FOREWORD

I met Chris Ward 20 years ago. We were both starting out in the restaurant world – he was working in the kitchen at Arthurs; I was waiting tables at the restaurant my mother owns, Mia's.

From the first time I met him, his passion for this business was apparent. You could hear the excitement in his voice when we talked food – and that's all we talked. You could tell even then, his love for cooking was going to be a lifelong commitment.

We kept in touch over the years. I knew he had become chef at the Pyramid Room and then heard he had gone to New Hampshire for awhile. In 1998, he was back in town and after only a few short meetings, we decided to become partners. (Strange as this may sound, earlier that year I etched on a prayer wall in Israel that we would do a restaurant together – and it came true.)

It's been a great decision. Not only is he perhaps the hardest working chef I've ever known, he is constantly challenging himself – testing ideas, searching for new flavor and food combinations, creating a wide variety of new dishes. He also reads more than any chef I know, devouring hundreds of cookbooks a year.

He may not know it, but I like to think of Chris as an example for today's young chefs who are working annonymously in the backs of kitchens just as he was 20 years ago, of what can be achieved with the right level of dedication and commitment.

Chris, I may be a business partner, but I'm also a big fan. And I'm even happier to call you a friend.

Mico
Mi Cocina Restaurants

P.S. Being in business with Chris has one perk that has given me an unexpected insight into his world. At The Mercury, there is a table in the exposed kitchen that puts me virtually in the middle of the action. I get to watch him make split second decisions on quality control while preparing multiple orders at the same time, obsessing with plate presentation and constantly tasting and re-tasting to make sure everything's perfect. It's like having front row tickets at an NBA game (I would say Chris is like Michael Jordon, but he's actually more like Larry Bird.)

A DAY IN MY RESTAURANT LIFE

12:35 a.m. Some nights I leave before midnight. Some nights I don't. It's amazing what has to be done before you can close up a restaurant – or in my case four. Like most chefs, I'm a perfectionist when it comes to having everything prepped correctly for the next day. That means checking on stocks, soups, sauce bases and hundreds of other little things. I just can't leave until everything is put away. (Tonight, as usual, I'm on the phone to the other three restaurants making sure they're ready to close, as well as ready to open the next day.)

The good news, it's just a short drive from my newest restaurant to my home. After a 16 hour day (as part of an 80 hour week), I actually enjoy these few minutes alone without the cell phone ringing, without someone coming to me with a question. I'm not complaining about the amount of work – I love it. But I'm at the age where I'm starting to feel it. At this pace, I may have only three to four more years putting in these kind of hours. But I will. I am determined that all of these restaurants will succeed.

At home, I'll wander around the house until 1:30 a.m. or so, unable to sleep, trying to decompress. In some ways, this is the best time of day – i.e. the only time of day – to think about menu changes, to read cookbooks (I've got four on my bed stand right now), to watch Fox News or Sports Center on ESPN.

I don't remember my dreams. But I'm sure I dream about food.

8:06 a.m.   I'm up. I'm up. I'm getting up. Just give me five more minutes.

8:46 a.m.   I'm at work most mornings before 9:00 a.m.. To get started, I need three things — a computer, a phone and iced tea. If you're around me for any length of time, you might wonder if that's all I drink. It usually is.

Being Executive Chef at four restaurants means four different types of headaches, but it usually ends up being the same two problems. Food and employees. While my computer lets me pull up daily reports on exactly how many guest we served last night at each restaurant, how much food was consumed, etc., I rely on my phone to get the real story. If the numbers don't make sense, I may call up the manager or the chef de cuisine (the chef in charge of each particular restaurant when I'm not there) and find out why we didn't make numbers or, on the other hand, why the numbers were so good.

Most mornings, though, I'm dealing with food issues. That means mentally juggling what's on order, what was ordered but didn't come in, and what did come in but is unacceptable. I usually double check to see if the organic micro-sprouts and mushrooms from Ohio got here. (We Fedex them in.) Then I'm on the phone trying to track down diver's scallops from Maine and black cod from Alaska. (Both are hard to get. Both are wonderful to cook. Both are incredible to eat.)

Food and food costs. Every day it's a different set of problems. My day's just started and all I'm thinking about are business issues. It's a bit jarring to tell you the truth. I'd rather think about cooking.

9:45 a.m.   By mid-morning, I'm usually meeting with the manager of the restaurant where I happen to be that day. I could be at Citizen near downtown, or at The Mercury Grill in north Dallas or at the newly opened restaurant, The Mercury in far north Dallas. (In a perfect world, I like to spend three consecutive days at each restaurant.) This is my time to address personnel issues and the rare – I'm happy to say – but inevitable customer complaints.

10:46 a.m.   Now for the first time today, I start to feel good. That's because I'm out of the office and in the kitchen. The business issues will have to wait. Now it's time for my last prep-check before lunch. I head straight to the line. (The 'line' is the area of my kitchens lined with grills, broilers, ovens and woks on one side and the food prep area, including steam and refrigerated tables on the other.) The line is where, to borrow a phrase, preparation meets opportunity. This is where the action is. At this time, I make sure, again, that vegetables have been blanched correctly, stocks are simmering, sauce bases are right, and the soups are in good shape.

11:35 a.m.   Sometimes I'll pause to watch the finishing prep work, and I generally have the same thought each time – the kitchen probably runs better without me here. While I'm certainly not 'in the way,' I disrupt things. I'm never content being an observer. I have to be a participant.

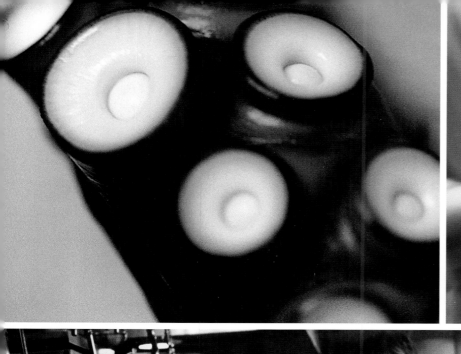

12: 22 p.m. Lunch has erupted. Not many people know this, but lunch for a chef can be more frenetic than dinner. It's compressed over a shorter period of time and every order has to be plated as quickly as possible. (There used to be a time when lunch was relaxed, but not in this economic environment.) Do I eat lunch? No. I find myself eating a crouton here, some french fries there, a bite of vegetable a bit later. And iced tea. Always iced tea. I never claimed to be an example of how to eat, just how to cook.

2:16 p.m. The restaurant is almost empty. This is usually when I have lunch with the General Manager. Well, at least he has lunch. I have iced tea. This is usually half business, half personal (we talk about the world, kids, guests who are regulars who showed up or who didn't show up).

As I'm sitting with my manager, it occurs to me: This is one of the reasons I'm a chef. I like sitting around a table with friends, family, and co-workers where I've cooked the food. I now realize that I was fortunate to be brought up in a family where my parents were passionate about all things culinary. My mother is a tremendous cook. Growing up in Shreveport, Louisiana, the best 'restaurant' in town was at my parents house. Mom and Dad introduced me to fine dining and everything that accompanied it — wine, caviar, the entire experience. While I had a very early interest in cooking, I had no overt desire to be a chef. It never crossed my mind. I just grew up normally. Played basketball in high school. Went off to college. But a $3.75 per hour summer job after my sophomore year changed everything. It was at the most popular restaurant in Dallas.

3:30 p.m. It's at this time of day I'm starting to lose a little energy. Some days I'll spend the entire day at one restaurant, other days I'm at all four over the course of a day. So jumping in my car and heading off to Citizen in the middle of the afternoon isn't unusual (it's the one restaurant that doesn't serve lunch). Talking on my cell phone the entire 30 minute drive isn't unusual either. I'm talking to my chef de cuisine at The Mercury to see how his lunch went and what problems he's facing for dinner. I'm calling purveyors or they're calling me. There really isn't a minute of peace.

The overall concept of Citizen (a Euro/Asian restaurant) had many influences. Nobu, a restaurant in New York offered a incredible example of what could be done

A DAY IN MY RESTAURANT LIFE **13**

Chris Ward
Executive Chef

(Nobu deserves all the acclaim he's received), but so too did a trip to Tokyo. After Tokyo, we knew that the sushi bar had to play a prominent role. The back of the house cuisine, prepared with European cooking techniques, would have to share equal 'billing' with a second to none sushi bar. That was our vision, and it works, in part because we have the proper staff who will settle for nothing less than perfection.

At first, I wasn't prepared for the fact that my $3.75 an hour job also demanded perfection. I started out at the appetizer station. Three and one half years later, I was the sous chef working 50 hours a week at one of the most popular restaurants in Dallas. (Sous chefs generally have to know how to work anywhere in the kitchen.) Somehow, while I was still going to school, everything in my life had changed. I now knew what I wanted to do. But it was dawning on me that as popular a restaurant as Arthur's was, I needed to move on, to experience a different kitchen. I got my wish.

Working at The Old Warsaw, in the early nineteen eighties, was as close as it came to working in Paris. First Giard Vullien, who had worked at Maxium's in Paris and then John Lafont were my chefs. Or should I say dictators. I floated throughout the kitchen, learning an immense amount, and swearing, that if I ever had my own restaurant, I would treat my staff differently. Here too, I realized I had set myself on a completely different course than my contemporaries. Friends who were now bankers or lawyers didn't stay up until three in the morning. It was my first real taste of the restaurant life, and I loved it.

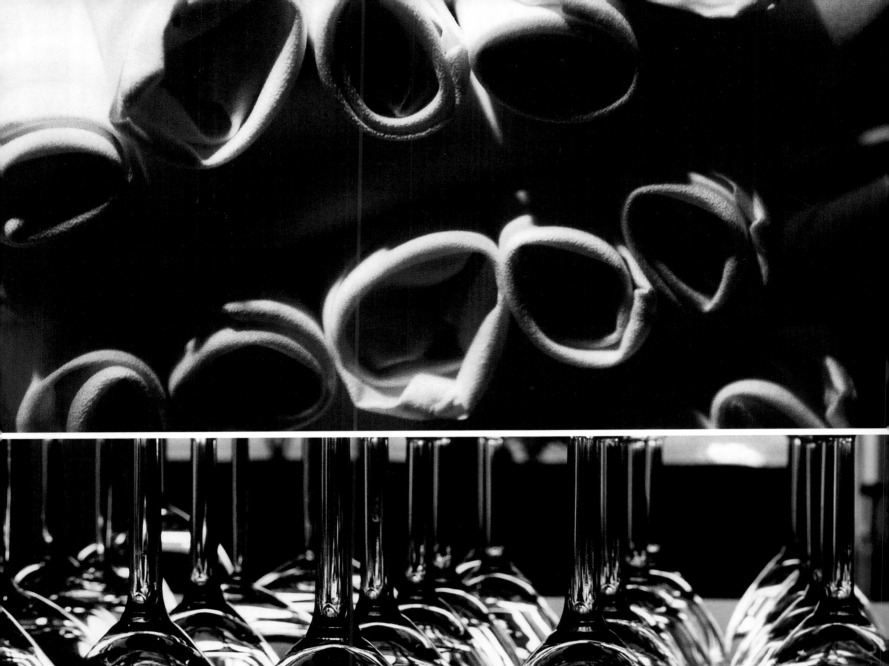

5:27 p.m. I've headed back to my newest restaurant, The Mercury, where I'm meeting with my chef de cuisine to discuss the evening specials. I allow my chefs a lot of latitude. Obviously I have veto power, but I want to see how their minds work (I usually suggest a twist or two for their ideas.) At this time of night, I meet with the servers and go over both the specials and any deletions or substitutions on the menu. I'll also take time to see how the back kitchen is set up – paying extra attention to see how the walk in refrigerators are arranged. Are things stored properly? Are we using perishables in the right order? I'm back to being the businessman, but just for a moment.

6:30 p.m. In the restaurant world, most executive chefs play the role of the 'expeditor.' The expeditor stands outside the line, calls the orders and fires the tickets. In English, this means that the executive chef acts somewhat as the conductor of the symphony, making sure the orders are being prepared how and when they should be and that the plate presentation is what it should be, too.

I can't do that. Or, perhaps I should say, I won't do that. I will not play the role of the expeditor. I have to be behind the line, in the middle of the action, actually cooking the dishes. From 6:30 to closing, for as long as it takes, I need to be physically preparing the food. I make no bones about it, I am a working chef.

When I thought I was ready to leave The Old Warsaw, I was hired to be the chef at a start up restaurant. To be charitable, I wasn't ready for the task and for a lot of reasons (some out of my control) the restaurant failed. I was becoming a good chef, but there is so much more to running a restaurant than just cooking. My next stop was at the Pyramid Room where I was the first American chef. From there I headed east to New Hampshire to be chef at the Beford Village Inn. While I loved the Inn, I missed Dallas. I had known Mico, now my business partner, years ago when he was waiting tables. In 1991, I had been one of his first customers when he opened his first restaurant (the first Mi Cocina). Somehow we stayed in touch over the years and in 1997 he contacted me with the idea of opening The Mercury (now named The Mercury Grill). It opened in 1998 in one of the most unlikely locations for an upscale restaurant – in a strip shopping center between a hair salon and a clothing consignment store.

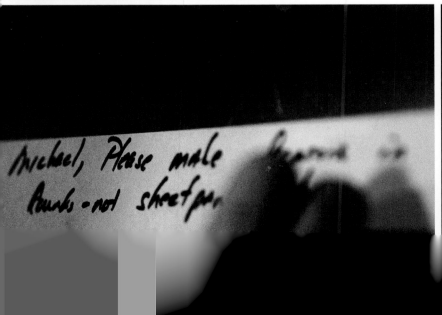

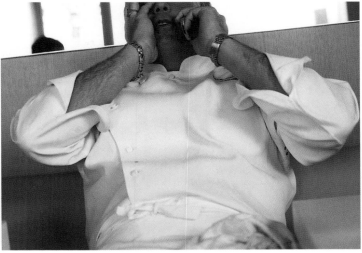

11:26 p.m. The last group of customers are about to leave. I think. I've been back in the walk-ins making mental notes about what I may need for tomorrow. I stop for a moment to look out over this new restaurant, the Mercury. It's an incredible space, painted almost all white but somehow managing to be both warm and cozy. The Mercury Grill, which opened first, is as dark as this is light. They were never meant to be part of a chain, but rather two restaurants 'connected' by slightly different versions of my French inspired new American cuisine.

But right now, I'm looking at my last customers of the day finishing their espresso and getting up to leave. I glance at my watch thinking what a great day this has been. I may get out of here before midnight.

BASICS & STOCKS

THE BACKBONE OF MY COOKING

"Stocks are recipes within recipes. Their importance can not be overstated. They add subtlety. They add flavor. They add texture. They are indispensible."

This may be difficult, but I'm going to try to convince you that stocks are worth getting excited about. I admit there's nothing particularly glamourous about them – the ingredients are as basic as it gets and to tell you the truth, they're a bit time-consuming to make. But I want to underscore this: there may be nothing in this entire book that will transform your cooking more than stocks. They are literally the backbone of my cooking. A good stock is the difference between just cooking food and creating great cuisine.

Stocks are recipes within recipes. They add subtlety. They add flavor. They add texture. Altogether, they are indispensible. (Not many people know this, but the bones used to make certain stocks add protein.) While the bad news is they may not be exciting to make, the good news is they are not hard to make. In fact, you'll find you have most of the ingredients on hand already.

Because they are the essential building blocks of my cooking, I rely on six or eight different stocks – veal (by far the most important), brown chicken, white chicken, vegetable, fish, shellfish and a few others. I hope I can convince you to work with just two or three.

When you become proficient at making stocks, when you're not afraid of making stocks (most of them freeze wonderfully, lasting two to three months), your confidence in the kitchen will soar.

Preparing these stocks may take extra work, but mastering the basic techniques is necessary before taking the next step in your cooking. When you start asking yourself, 'what stock do I need to get started for this recipe?,' then you're getting to be as passionate about cooking as I. (O.K., maybe I'm a tad bit more passionate, but you're headed in the right direction.)

The basics make all the other sections possible. This is why I have put the stock section at the front of the book.

LOBSTER STOCK

Very rarely do we make fish stock at any of the restaurants. I find that the subtle sweetness of a lobster stock lends a more agreeable flavor than a stock made from simple scraps of fish bone. You can leave out the tarragon, but I think it rounds out the flavors. This stock doesn't reduce well for storage; the flavor goes south. You're better off either making it fresh as the recipe calls for it, or freezing at full strength for no longer than 1 month.

Heat the oil in a 3-gallon stockpot over high heat until it begins to smoke. Add the lobster shells. Stir the shells until they turn red, about 5 minutes. Reduce the heat to medium, add the tomatoes, carrot, onion, celery, leek and garlic and continue to cook for 20-30 minutes, stirring occasionally. Remove the pan from the heat and add the brandy and vermouth. Return pot to heat and reduce the liquid by about 2/3. Cover the lobster shells and vegetables with 1-1/2 gallons of water. Add the peppercorns, thyme and bay leaves. Simmer for 30 minutes over low heat, skimming the sauce when the fat comes to the surface. Pass the stock through a fine strainer, add the tarragon and simmer for 15 minutes more. Remove the tarragon, restrain and chill. The finished stock should be slightly cloudy with a pinkish orange tinge.

This stock will keep for 4 days in the refrigerator and 1 month in the freezer.

INGREDIENTS

1/2 cup vegetable oil

6 lobster heads, roughly cut up with a cleaver

10 tomatoes, halved

1 carrot, peeled and chopped

1 onion, chopped

2 ribs of celery, chopped

1 leek, cleaned and chopped

2 heads of garlic, halved

2 cups dry vermouth

1 cup brandy

1 teaspoon black peppercorns

1 bunch fresh thyme

2 bay leaves

1/2 bunch of fresh tarragon or mint marigold, tied with string

BROWN VEAL STOCK

If you only make one stock, take the time to make this one. (It's the only veal stock I make and it's worth its weight in gold.) With this one stock, you can make many of the recipes in this book. Use veal bones (not beef bones) especially the knuckle. The process of browning the bones gives a richness that is key to bringing a so-so stock to greater heights of flavor. All stocks are brought to a simmer but never boiled. This assures clarity. This stock can be frozen for up to 3 months.

Preheat the oven to 450°. Place the veal bones in a large roasting pan and drizzle 3 tablespoons vegetable oil over them. Roast for 3 hours or until nicely browned, turning the bones every 30 minutes to extract the every bit of flavor essence from them. Remove bones and place in a 3-gallon stock pot.

Add the onions, celery and carrots to the roasting pan, return to the oven and roast the vegetables until they lightly caramelize, about 25 – 30 minutes. At this stage, you will see a light brown char on some of the edges of the veggies. Stir in the tomato paste

INGREDIENTS

10 pounds veal bones

3 tablespoons vegetable oil

3 onions, peeled and roughly chopped

1 rib celery, roughly chopped

2 carrots, roughly chopped

2 heads garlic, halved

4 bay leaves

1/2 level teaspoon whole cloves

1 tablespoon black peppercorns

6 sprigs fresh thyme

1 cup tomato paste

and cook for an additional 45 minutes, stirring every 15. Don't be alarmed if the tomato paste blackens, that's the natural sugar in the paste and it will add yet another layer of flavor to the stock. Remove the vegetables and the bones from the pan and add them to the stockpot. Add 2 cups of water to the roasting pan and scrape up all the "drippings". If you have a hard time getting all the bits up, place the pan on the stove and warm it over two burners, then slowly scrape. Add this elixir to the stockpot and fill the pot with cold water to cover. Add the herbs and the garlic. Simmer for 8-10 hours over very low heat (overnight works very well). Skim the fat from the surface of the stock every chance you get. After 10 hours, strain the stock into a container and allow to cool slightly. Store immediately. If you are going to use the stock within a few days, store it in the refrigerator. Any unused stock may be frozen in freezer bags or plastic storage containers. Use within 2 months.

Demi-Glace: Gently simmer the strained stock, reducing the contents by 1/2. This will keep, refrigerated, for about 1 week or frozen for up to 3 months.

Glace de Viande: Return the bones and vegetables to the stockpot. Fill the pot with water to cover and bring to a boil. Immediately turn down the heat and simmer for an additional 8-10 hours. Strain this stock and return the liquid to a clean, smaller pot. Reduce over medium heat until it reaches a black syrupy consistency. Strain again and refrigerate. It will keep for about a month, well covered in the refrigerator. Although the yield is a mere 1/2 cup, you waste absolutely nothing.
This ultra-condensed veal glaze goes a long way toward enhancing a sauce or soup.

Variations: Use the same method as for the Veal Stock except use game bones, such as venison, elk, pigeon or quail. Deglaze the roasting pan with 1 cup of red wine vinegar and 1 cup water instead of the 2 cups water.

VEGETABLE STOCK

In the last few years, the use of this stock has become more prominent in my kitchens (in The Mercury we may go through 30 to 40 gallons per week). This stock is a good substitute for chicken stock in soups. If you are making a heartier soup, roast the vegetables as you would the bones in a brown stock. You can get a little creative here — maybe a few halves of sun-dried tomato, parsley juice or a small bulb of fennel. I also use vegetable stock to make risotto.

Place all the ingredients in a 3-gallon stock pot. Add 2-1/2 gallons of cool water and bring to a simmer. Cook for 30-40 minutes. Strain the liquid and chill immediately. Vegetable stock will keep in the refrigerator for 5-6 days or frozen for 1 month.

INGREDIENTS

2 yellow onions, peeled and roughly chopped

2 ribs celery, roughly chopped

1 carrot, peeled and roughly chopped

1 whole leek, cleaned and roughly chopped

2 whole tomatoes, halved

2 cups mushroom pieces or stems

1 turnip, peeled and diced

1 bunch parsley

1 bunch fresh thyme

1 sprig rosemary

2 cloves garlic, peeled

4 bay leaves

1 tablespoon black peppercorns

2 cups dry vermouth

WHITE CHICKEN STOCK

This is a mild flavored, neutral stock that is used in making soups as well as 'finishing' a sauce during service. Adding chicken stock at the proper time adds a little finesse or 'umph' to a dish. It is also used in many pasta dishes and in certain risottos.

Place the chicken bones, vegetables, spices and herbs in a 3-gallon stockpot. Fill the pot with cool water. Place on the stove and heat to a simmer. Cook for 4-6 hours, constantly skimming the fat and scum that accumulates on the surface. Don't boil the stock or it will become cloudy. Strain the stock into a container and allow to cool slightly. Store immediately. This stock can be refrigerated for 4-6 days and will freeze well for up to 1 month.

INGREDIENTS

3 pounds uncooked chicken bones or the carcasses from 3 cleaned whole chickens

2 white onions, peeled and roughly chopped

2 carrots, peeled and roughly chopped

1 leek, cleaned and roughly chopped

1/2 rib celery, roughly chopped

1 bunch fresh parsley

1 bunch fresh thyme

3 bay leaves

1 clove garlic

2 or 3 whole cloves

1 teaspoon black peppercorns

BROWN CHICKEN STOCK

Browning the bones gives a rich flavor and a dark color to this stock. Brown chicken stock is similar to veal stock, but with an intense chicken flavor. I use this stock for sauces that go with fowl.

Preheat the oven to 425°. Heat a roasting pan with the oil and when the oil begins to smoke add the chicken bones and brown them, turning frequently. Add the onion, celery, carrots, and tomato paste, mixing them in with the bones. Return the pan to the oven. Continue to cook until the vegetables are browned, about 45 minutes, stirring occasionally.

Remove the pan from the oven and place the contents in a large stockpot. Add the water, herbs, pepper and garlic. Bring to a simmer and cook for 4-6 hours. Strain the stock into a container and allow to cool slightly. Store immediately. This stock can be refrigerated for 4-6 days and will freeze well for up to 1 month.

INGREDIENTS

2 tablespoons vegetable oil

2 pounds uncooked chicken bones
(or the carcasses from 2 cleaned whole chickens)

1 onion, peeled and roughly cut

2 ribs celery, chopped

1 carrot, peeled and roughly cut

1 cup tomato paste

1 head garlic, cut in 1/2 horizontally

1 teaspoon whole black peppercorn

2 bay leaves

1 sprig fresh thyme

4 quarts cool water

FISH ESSENCE

Years ago, this stock or 'essence' was a mainstay in classic French cooking (used in poaching fish, for example). Today, because of it's intense flavor – and due to the fact that I prefer steaming or sautéing fish – it is used much more sparingly. Where it is called for in a recipe, you could substitute diluted clam broth.

Soak the fish bones in cold water overnight. Soaking will release the blood from the fish bones resulting in a clearer fish fumé. Drain the water from the bones and place a 1-1/2 to 2-gallon stockpot on the stove. Add the oil and when the oil begins to smoke add the drained fish bones. Stir the bones around until they whiten in color. Add the onion, celery, leek, parsley and the garlic, cooking until they are soft. Add the white wine and reduce by two-thirds. Add the water and the herbs. Bring the stock to a simmer, skimming off the fat that comes to the surface. Simmer for 30 minutes. Strain the stock into a container and allow to cool slightly. Store immediately. The next day the stock should have a silky, gelatinous quality. Stock can be refrigerated for 3-4 days and will freeze well for up to 1 month.

INGREDIENTS

3 tablespoons vegetable oil

2 pounds fish bones, broken into at least 4 sections

1 medium yellow onion, peeled and diced

2 stalks celery, roughly cut into a large dice

1 large leek, cleaned and cut into a large dice

1 bunch Italian flat leaf parsley

2 cloves garlic

1 bay leaf

1 sprig fresh thyme

1 cup white wine

2 1/2 quarts cool water

MUSHROOM STOCK

Makes 1-1/2 quarts

Any peelings and stems from mushrooms such as morels, chanterelles, crimini, button, yellow foot or trumpet will do nicely in this stock. I do not recommend Shiitake or portobellos; their distinct flavor doesn't blend well with that of the others. This stock is primarily used in soups and certain risottos.

Heat the oil on high in a large pot. When it begins to smoke add the mushroom pieces and sauté for 4-5 minutes. Add onion, celery, shallots and cook for 5 minutes more. Deglaze the pot by adding the vermouth and stirring with a large metal spoon to dislodge the darkened bits. Add the bay leaf, thyme and water. Simmer for 1 hour. Strain stock into a container and allow to cool for about 30 minutes. Store immediately. Stock can be refrigerated for 4-6 days and will freeze well for up to 1 month.

INGREDIENTS

1 tablespoon vegetable oil

4 cups assorted mushroom peelings

1 medium onion, peeled and roughly cut

1 rib celery, roughly cut

2 shallots, peeled and roughly cut

1 fresh bay leaf

2 sprigs of fresh thyme

1 cup dry vermouth

2 quarts cool water

BASIC PESTO

Makes 1 cup

In a food processor or blender combine the basil, garlic, salt and pepper. Pulse the machine to chop the leaves. Add the cheese and pine nuts and purée until almost smooth. With the machine running, gradually add the oil in a slow stream until the mixture is a blended paste.

INGREDIENTS

2 cups basil leaves, lightly packed

3 garlic cloves

1/2 teaspoon kosher salt

1/2 teaspoon freshly ground black pepper

1/2 cup Parmigiano-Reggiano cheese

1/4 cup pine nuts

1/2 cup extra virgin olive oil

PASTA DOUGH

TO MAKE BY HAND

Mix both the flours and salt together on a clean work surface. Make a well in the center and add the eggs. Slowly, using your fingertips, incorporate the eggs into the flour until the mixture begins to form a mealy ball. Knead the ball of dough for 3-5 minutes until it becomes firm and glossy in appearance. Wrap tightly in plastic and rest for at least one hour.

TO MAKE BY MACHINE

Place all ingredients in electric mixer with the dough hook attached. Mix dough at a low speed for 10 minutes or until it is smooth and silky. Cover with plastic and reserve until ready to use.

INGREDIENTS

8 whole eggs, beaten

6 cups all purpose flour

2 cups Durham flour

1 tablespoon kosher salt

BALSAMIC VINAIGRETTE

Makes 1/2 cup

Whisk the shallots, vinegar and olive oil together with a fork. Season to taste with salt and pepper. This dressing will keep for 2 weeks, refrigerated.

INGREDIENTS

1/2 teaspoon finely chopped shallots

2 tablespoons balsamic vinegar

1/2 cup extra virgin olive oil

Salt and freshly ground black pepper

BAKING POWDER BISCUITS

These light, airy biscuits have been a part of my family's cooking heritage for a very long time. As long as I can remember, they have always been there at Thanksgiving and Christmas dinners. The holidays wouldn't be the same without them.

Mix all the ingredients except the milk with a pastry cutter until the dough begins to ball together. Do not overwork the mixture. If the dough is over-worked you will have a tough, heavy biscuit. Gradually add the milk. Remove the dough and place on a lightly floured surface. Roll the dough to 1/2" to 2/3" thickness and cut the biscuits out with 2" diameter cutter that has been dipped in flour to alleviate sticking. Place on an ungreased baking sheet and cook for 20-25 minutes, until nicely browned. Remove from oven and serve warm.

INGREDIENTS

3 cups flour

1/4 to 1/3 cup milk

2 1/2 tablespoons sugar

4 1/2 teaspoons baking powder

1 teaspoon salt

1 1/2 sticks cold butter, cut into small pieces

HORS D'OEUVRES

"Rather than putting

them on a cracker,

I like to pass a tray that

has the hors d'oeuvres

placed in individual

spoons."

Hors d'oeuvres are a pain. Most chefs would rather make anything else. Hors d'oeuvres aren't usually served in restaurants. They are usually reserved for catering events. I feel that hors d'oeuvres present the classic catering problem – how do you keep the quality, temperature, and appearance consistent over a large number of servings. Plus, you put in all of that effort and it's gone in one bite.

You can become very creative making hors d'oeuvres. They can also become very time-consuming to prepare. The usage of ingredients for hors d'oeuvres is endless, from simple ingredients such as cheese, bread, tomatoes, to exotic ingredients such as caviar, foie gras, or toro tuna.

One of my favorite things to do with hors d'oeuvres is to change the way they're presented. For example, rather than putting them on a cracker, I like to pass a tray that has the hors d'oeuvres placed in individual spoons. My point is, have some fun with this.

Among all the recipes in this section, I want to draw your attention to one in particular: the Ricotta and Anchovy Canapés. Ricotta cheese is usually purchased but in this book you learn to make it. Believe me, it's simple to make and you will never again be satisfied with anything less than freshly made ricotta. Besides the canapes, you can find a variety of other uses for your ricotta. Almost every Italian red dish – lasagna, manicotti, etc. – is dramatically improved by using your own ricotta. It's mild, it's subtle, and you and your family (or guests) will taste the difference immediately.

QUENELLE OF FRESH RICOTTA
with Shrimp and Basil Mint Pesto on Grilled Sourdough Bruschetta

I don't you think can really appreciate ricotta cheese until you make it yourself (and once you've tried fresh ricotta, you'll never go back to store bought). Fresh ricotta is relatively easy to make.

TO MAKE THE PESTO
Place all the ingredients in a blender or food processor until you have a coarse but compact mixture. Taste for salt and pepper and store in the refrigerator. This can be stored in the refrigerator for up to one week left in a covered container with a thin layer of olive oil on top. If you don't want use additional oil, you can press a piece of plastic wrap onto the surface, changing the film each time you use it.

TO MAKE THE QUENELLE MIXTURE
Stir the Parmigiano-Reggiano into the ricotta and reserve at room temperature.

TO MAKE THE BRUSCHETTA
Brush the large bruschetta of sourdough with the olive oil. Toast on the grill on both sides. Rub the toast on both sides with the garlic. Spread with a little pesto. Reserve.

TO MAKE THE QUENELLE AND ASSEMBLY
Using 2 oval shaped tablespoons, pick up a spoonful of the ricotta mixture and with the second spoon, scrape a side of the ricotta letting the mixture fall into the second spoon. Repeat this process until you have a 3-sided oval-shaped quenelle. Place the quenelle on the prepared bruschetta, wedging a shrimp against the quenelle. Garnish with a shaved curl of the asiago cheese.

MISE EN PLACE:

1/2 cup Basil Mint Pesto (recipe follows)

Ricotta Quenelle (recipe follows)

Large slice of sourdough bread, cut 1/2" thick

1 tablespoon extra virgin olive oil

1 clove garlic, cut in 1/2

3 cooked shrimp (10-12 count)

Curls of asiago cheese for garnish, shaved with a vegetable peeler

FOR THE PESTO:

2 bunches fresh basil, leaves only

3/4 - 1 ounce fresh mint, leaves only (a good fistful)

1 bunch Italian flat leaf parsley, leaves only

1 cup extra virgin olive oil

1/2 cup Parmigiano-Reggiano cheese

FOR THE RICOTTA QUENELLE:

6 ounces fresh ricotta (see page 34)

1 ounce Parmigiano-Reggiano cheese

RICOTTA AND ANCHOVY CANAPÉS

If you want to know what I think about fresh ricotta, please read the previous recipe introduction.

TO MAKE

Preheat the oven to 400°. If the ricotta is very moist, wrap it in cheesecloth and let drain in a sieve set over a large bowl for 30 minutes.

In a food processor puree the ricotta, anchovies, butter, olive oil and pepper to taste.

Place the bread slices on a baking sheet and toast for 2-3 minutes until lightly browned. Alternately, toast bread in a toaster.

Trim the crusts off the toasted bread and quarter each slice. Spread the ricotta paste on the toast squares, garnish with a leaf of flat leaf parsley and serve at room temperature.

If these are going to sit out for more than 30 minutes, cover with a barely damp paper towel.

INGREDIENTS

1/2 cup ricotta cheese (recipe follows)

4 anchovy fillets, fresh or salted

1/2 tablespoon of unsalted butter, room temperature

1 1/2 teaspoon extra virgin olive oil

Freshly ground pepper

7 slices of thinly sliced firm textured white bread

PECORINO AND FRESH MINT CANAPÉS

Serves 4

While I prefer that you would use pecorino cheese in this recipe, you can substitute Parmigiano-Reggiano. The difference is that pecorino is a tad saltier than Parmigiano-Reggiano. Both are excellent.

TO MAKE

Put cheese in a small bowl. Slowly pour in the oil, stirring with a fork. Stir in the cream. Mix in the chopped mint and season with salt and pepper. Spread the cheese on the bread, top each cube with a mint leaf and serve.

INGREDIENTS

1/4 cup freshly grated Pecorino

1 1/2 tablespoons extra virgin olive oil

1 tablespoon heavy cream

8 fresh mint leaves, chopped, plus 12 smaller leaves for garnish

salt and freshly ground pepper

12-2" cubes of peasant bread

FRESH RICOTTA

The flavor of homemade ricotta is full and sweet. It cannot be duplicated by buying it at the store. I'll say it again: make it at home and it will be the only ricotta you will ever eat.

In a non-reactive pot, heat the half & half and cream to a boil, stirring occasionally. Just before it comes to a boil, the surface will start to steam. You want to remove the pan from the heat at the moment that the steam becomes profuse, seconds before it boils. Off the heat, add the buttermilk, stirring slowly until you can see the mixture begin to curdle. Put the pot back on the heat and cook for 3 minutes, giving it an occasional slow stir. The mixture should start to curdle. Strain this mixture through a fine strainer. What accumulates in the strainer will look somewhat like a fine-curded cottage cheese. At this point, the cheese has a high moisture content. If you prefer it drier, place the strainer in a bowl, cover all with plastic film and let it drain in the refrigerator overnight. Season the cheese with kosher salt to taste, folding it in with a rubber spatula.

INGREDIENTS

2 cups half & half

2 cups heavy cream

1 cup buttermilk

Other chefs have tried wrapping shrimp in many things, but I really like this solution – kataifi. This gives it the look of pasta with the taste of phyllo with a very appealing crunch.

In a food processor combine the mayonnaise, lemon juice, vinegar, soy sauce and ginger. Process in long pulses until smooth. With the machine on, gradually drizzle in the olive oil. Add the cabbage, scraping down the sides as necessary until coarsely chopped. Season to taste with salt and pepper. Transfer the relish to a bowl, cover and refrigerate. The relish can be prepared up to one day in advance. Remove it from the refrigerator 30 minutes before serving.

In a large saucepan heat the vegetable oil over moderately high heat to 350°. Meanwhile in a medium bowl toss the flour with 1/3 teaspoon each salt and pepper. Add the shrimp and toss to coat, shaking off the excess. Set aside.

In a medium bowl beat the eggs with fork, pull the Kataifi apart into strands and place in bowl. Dip each shrimp in the eggs, then coat well with the Kataifi, pressing it gently onto the shrimp with your hands.

Fry shrimp 3 at a time in the hot oil, turning several times until golden and cooked through, about 3 minutes. Drain on paper towels and sprinkle lightly with salt.

ASSEMBLY
Divide relish between 4 plates. Place 3 shrimp on top. Serve hot.

INGREDIENTS

1/3 cup mayonnaise

2 tablespoons fresh lemon juice

1 tablespoon red wine vinegar

1 1/2 teaspoons soy sauce

2 thin coins of peeled fresh ginger

2 tablespoons olive oil

3 cups thinly sliced red cabbage

salt and freshly ground pepper

1 quart vegetable oil for frying

1/2 cup all purpose flour

12 large tiger shrimp or prawns (1 pound) shelled and deveined

2 eggs

1/3 of a 1 pound box of Kataifi

These spring rolls are light, cool and refreshing – perfect for dipping in either a peanut or sweet and sour sauce. We serve them at Citizen, our Euro/Asian restaurant that combines asian ingredients with classic French cooking techniques.

TO MAKE THE SHRIMP

Place all of the ingredients except the shrimp in a pot. Bring to a boil, reduce the heat and simmer for 10 minutes. Then place the shrimp in the water and cook for 2 1/2 minutes just until opaque. Remove the shrimp the water and chill them as quickly as possible. When the shrimp are cold, cut them in half lengthwise and reserve chilled.

ASSEMBLY

The spring rolls need to be assembled one at a time. Have all your ingredients close at hand. Pour the warm water in a bowl, dip one of the rice papers in the warm water until it becomes soft and pliable. Remove from the water and line the inside of the paper with a leaf of Boston lettuce. Place two shrimp halves on the lettuce, then place 10-12 bean sprouts on top of the shrimp. Place 6 carrot pieces on the bean sprouts and add a 1/4 ounce cellophane noodles (about 1/8 cup or so) on top. Sprinkle the basil, mint and cilantro over the noodles. Begin to roll up the ingredients, halfway fold in the 2 ends and continue to roll until you have a cylinder. Refrigerate until ready to serve.

INGREDIENTS

8 cooked shrimp (recipe follows)

6 ounces cellophane noodles or rice vermicelli, soaked in warm water until soft

8 square rice papers

8 inner leaves of Boston lettuce

3 ounces bean sprouts

8 fresh basil leaves - preferably Thai basil

10 fresh mint leaves

1/2 bunch of cilantro, leaves only

1/2 medium carrot, peeled and cut into julienne

1 quart of very hot water

FOR THE SHRIMP

1/2 medium onion, peeled and roughly cut

1/2 rib celery, roughly cut

1/2 teaspoon black peppercorns

1 lemon, cut in half

1 bay leaf

1 quart water

8 jumbo shrimp, (16/20 count) peeled and deveined with the tail shells removed

EGGPLANT CAVIAR *with Country Bread*

Refreshing garlic-tomato dip that can be used as a topping for fish as well as bread (in fact, the uses are endless). I call this dish eggplant 'caviar' due to the seeds that are left in that resemble black and white caviar.

Preheat the oven at 350°. Brush the eggplant halves with 1 tablespoon of the olive oil and place them on a baking sheet, cut sides down. Bake 45 minutes or until the skin is wrinkled and the flesh is tender when pierced. Remove from the oven and let cool.

Meanwhile, in a medium skillet heat 1 tablespoon of the olive oil over moderate heat. Once hot, add the scallions, bell pepper, jalapeño. Cook, stirring occasionally until softened, about 5 minutes. Scrape the vegetables into a medium bowl and set aside. Add the mushrooms to the skillet and cook until softened and the moisture has evaporated, 5-7 minutes. Set aside to cool.

Scoop the eggplant flesh onto a work surface, discarding the skins. Finely chop the eggplant and mushrooms. Add to the cooked vegetables in the bowl. Stir in the tomato, basil, 2 1/2 tablespoons chives, 1 1/2 teaspoons garlic and the remaining 2 tablespoons oil. Cover and refrigerate. The dip can be prepared to this point up to 1 day ahead.

Preheat the oven to 400°. Toss the bread chunks with the remaining 1/2 teaspoon garlic and toast on a baking sheet for about 10 minutes, turning once until golden brown.

Season the eggplant dip with salt and pepper. Mound it in a bowl and garnish with minced chives, serve the toast chunks in a basket on the side.

INGREDIENTS

2-3 medium eggplants (3 pounds) halved lengthwise

1/4 cup olive oil

5 scallions, white portion only, thinly sliced

1 medium red bell pepper cut in 1/8" dice

1/2 small jalapeño pepper, seeded and minced, or 1 pinch of cayenne pepper

1/4 pound mushrooms thinly sliced

1 large tomato - peeled, seeded and cut in 1/8" dice

1/3 cup (packed) fresh basil leaves, finely chopped

2 1/2 tablespoons finely minced chives, plus a little more for garnish

2 teaspoons minced garlic

1 small loaf of country bread, cut in small chunks

salt and freshly ground pepper

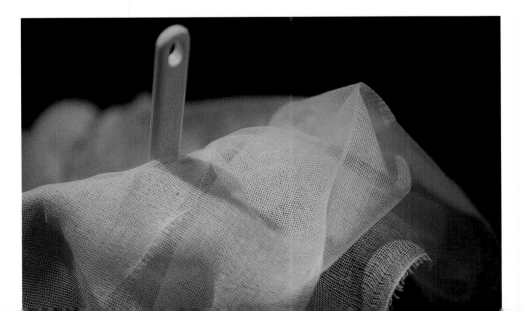

APPETIZERS

"I love experimenting, letting my imagination run wild – combining tastes, textures and temperatures in unusual and surprising ways."

There's an old French saying, "The appetite comes with the eating." That describes the purpose of an appetizer, or 'first course' perfectly. It should wake up your palate, give you a taste of what is to come, to make you hungry for more.

For me, appetizers are a secret love. That's because I love experimenting, letting my imagination run wild – combining tastes, textures and temperatures in unusual and surprising ways.

I know for most of you, preparing appetizers at home isn't really an option (with the exception of perhaps your most formal dinners). But just try preparing one dish for the entire family and let everyone have a bite. Add a soup or salad and you have a light meal.

My hope is that even if you don't prepare many appetizers at home, you'll come to appreciate the hidden role they play in restaurants – giving you an insight into how a chef thinks. (And, more importantly, appetizers let you judge whether he or she is a risk taker whose risk taking pays off.)

When I'm thinking of new appetizers, one of my favorite tactics is combining two intense flavors that are traditionally served separately. They need to be flavors that can stand on their own. For example, one of my recent creations marries foie gras with kobe beef (see the Foie Gras chapter). I admittedly this is an overpowering combination of flavors and ordering it is clearly an example of indulging yourself, but sometimes you should indulge yourself a little. You can't eat much of this dish, it's just too rich (speaking of rich, that's the other reason this dish is not served as an entree – the cost would be prohibitive).

JAVA-CURED BEEF
in a Parmesan Crisp with an Almost Caesar Salad

An adaptation of Caesar salad – topped with warm java-cured beef.

TO MAKE THE JAVA CURE
Cut the top off the garlic heads so all the cloves are slightly exposed. Lightly brush the garlic with oil and grill until soft and lightly browned. Alternately, the heads can be wrapped in foil and roasted for 1 hour in a 350° oven. Squeeze the soft garlic out of the pods and into a blender with the rest of the ingredients. Purée until smooth. Both this step and the next can be done a day ahead.

TO MAKE THE CHEESE CRISP
Preheat oven to 400°. Spray a couple of cookie sheets with oil. Sprinkle about 1-1/2 tablespoons of the cheese into a circle about 4-inches in diameter. Make 2 circles per sheet. Overlap the baking of each pan so you will be able to shape the crisps before the others have a chance to cool. Bake until they melt and turn a golden brown, about 3-4 minutes. The smell in the kitchen will dramatically increase as the cheese browns. Remove the pan from the oven and carefully remove a disk with a spatula. Place the disk smooth side down over a small glass bowl or coffee cup, pressing lightly so the disk conforms to the shape of the bowl. Do the same with the rest of the disks and allow to cool and harden. To reserve, place in an airtight container separated with paper toweling.

TO MAKE THE SALAD DRESSING
Purée the egg yolk, mustard, garlic, anchovy, Worcestershire sauce and vinegar in a blender until smooth. Pour into a bowl and slowly whisk in the vegetable and olive oils. Add the lemon juice and the cheese. Season with salt and pepper to taste. Chill.

TO MAKE THE BEEF
Portion the beef into 4 equal portions and pour the marinade over all. Marinate for at least 4 hours. Preheat the grill for high heat. Remove the meat from the marinade scraping the marinade off with your fingers and grill for 1 – 2 minutes on each side for medium rare. Allow meat to rest for 5 minutes. Cut each mignon into 1/4"slices.

TO ASSEMBLE
Place a parmesan cup in the center of a warm serving plate. Lightly toss the julienne of Romaine with enough Caesar salad dressing to coat the lettuce. Place equal amounts of the salad in the parmesan crisps. Place each group of mignon slices on top of the Caesar salad. Top with shaved parmesan cheese and freshly cracked black pepper.

MISE EN PLACE

12 ounces beef tenderloin

Java Cure (recipe follows)

Parmesan Crisp (recipe follows)

Almost Caesar Salad (recipe follows)

FOR THE JAVA CURE

6 heads roasted garlic

2 tablespoons extra virgin olive oil

1 1/2 tablespoons freshly ground coffee

1 1/2 teaspoons kosher salt

2 1/2 tablespoons maple syrup

1/4 cup water

FOR THE PARMESAN CRISP

1/4 cup grated Parmigiano-Reggiano cheese

FOR THE ALMOST CAESAR SALAD

1 head romaine lettuce, rinsed and cut into a julienne

1 egg yolk

1 teaspoon Dijon mustard

3 cloves garlic

1 anchovy

1/2 teaspoon Worcestershire sauce

2 tablespoons red wine vinegar

1/4 cup vegetable oil

1/4 cup extra virgin olive oil

Juice of 1 lemon

1 tablespoon Parmigiano-Reggiano cheese

salt and pepper

SPECIAL EQUIPMENT

4 small glass bowls or coffee cups

TUNA TARTAR ON CHARDONNAY

This is an easy and fun way to create a memorable presentation. It only requires a few items: ruby-red sushi grade tuna for the tartar, a quail egg and baked sour dough slices all placed – literally – over a glass of Chardonnay. It looks good enough to eat and drink.

TO MAKE THE CROUTON

Preheat the oven to 375°. Place the slices of sourdough on a cookie sheet. Drizzle the bread with extra virgin olive oil and bake until lightly browned and crisp, about 5 minutes.

TO MAKE THE QUAIL EGG

Gently place the 4 quail eggs in simmering water and cook for 4 minutes. When done, place the eggs in cold water to stop the cooking process. Peel the eggs, cover with a damp cloth and keep cool.

TO MAKE THE TARTAR

Place the tuna, parsley, ginger, mint, cumin, shallots and olive oil in a non-reactive bowl and toss well. Season with lime juice, salt and pepper to taste.

TO ASSEMBLE

Pour equal amounts of chardonnay in 4 wine glasses. Brush the bottoms of the croutons, removing excess crumbs. Divide the tartar into equal amounts and place on top of each crouton. At this point, it's easier to take the glasses and the croutons to where you are going to serve them and assemble them there. About 10 minutes before serving, fill each glass with chardonnay about 1/3 to 1/2 full. Carefully place a prepared crouton on top of each glass. Place a peeled quail egg on top of the tartar and serve immediately. This hors d'oeuvre can sit out for about 30 to 40 minutes, no more.

MISE EN PLACE

4 slices sourdough bread, cut 1/8" thick

4 quail eggs (optional)

Tuna Tartar (recipe follows)

Good quality, fruity chardonnay

SPECIAL EQUIPMENT

4 white wine glasses

FOR THE TUNA TARTAR

6 ounces sushi grade tuna
cut into a 1/4" dice

1 tablespoon chopped Italian parsley

1/2 teaspoon chopped fresh ginger

1/2 teaspoon chopped fresh mint

1 pinch cumin

2 tablespoons extra virgin olive oil

1 teaspoon chopped shallots

lime juice to taste

salt and pepper to taste

One of my biggest sellers at the restaurant (it has received overwhelming acclaim) and the truth is, I put it on the menu as an afterthought. This simple dish helped make The Mercury's reputation and as long as I'm in business, it will always be on the menu.

TO MAKE THE COUSCOUS

Bring 2 quarts water and the salt to a rolling boil. Add couscous, cook 5-6 minutes or until al dente. Strain the cooked couscous under cold water until chilled; gently toss with 2 tablespoons vegetable oil. Place in a container and refrigerate.

TO MAKE THE VINAIGRETTE

Bring the water and truffle peelings to a boil. Place both in a blender. Slowly add the olive oil. (Note: if the truffles are not hot the oil will not emulsify and you will have a broken vinaigrette.) Slowly add the rice wine vinegar and then the black truffle oil. Season with salt and pepper to taste and reserve in a cool place.

TO POACH THE EGGS

Boil quart of water and 1 cup white vinegar. Season the water with salt. Place eggs in the boiling water and cook 3-4 minutes for a soft poach. Remove the eggs from the water and place on top of the couscous when plating (see below).

TO MAKE COUSCOUS CARBONARA

Sauté the cooked bacon, cream and cooked couscous together. After the cream begins to boil add the grated cheese. Reduce until the cream begins to coat the pearl couscous. Add the butter, chives and tomatoes and mix well. Reserve in a warm place.

ASSEMBLY

Spoon equal portions of the couscous mixture onto 4 plates. Place a heated poached egg on top. Gently drizzle the black truffle vinaigrette around the couscous and serve.

MISE EN PLACE

Pearl Couscous (recipe follows)

2 ounces Applewood bacon, diced and cooked crisp

1 1/4 cups heavy cream

4 ounces Parmigiano-Reggiano cheese, grated

2 ounces unsalted butter

1 1/2 tablespoons chopped chives

2 tablespoons diced tomato concassé

Truffle Vinaigrette (recipe follows)

4 large eggs

FOR THE PEARL COUSCOUS

1 pound Israeli pearl couscous

2 tablespoons kosher salt

2 tablespoons vegetable oil

FOR THE VINAIGRETTE

1 1/2 tablespoons chopped truffles, canned peelings may be substituted

1/2 cup water

1/4 cup rice wine vinegar

1/2 cup extra virgin olive oil

1 tablespoons black truffle oil

salt and freshly ground pepper

IMPERIAL ROLLS

The wrappers mentioned in this recipe are Thai or Vietnamese wrappers, not Chinese. They fry better. One key to this recipe is to work the pork until it has a smooth texture.

Mix all of the ingredients except for the wrappers, in an electric mixer with a paddle attachment. Mix on low speed for 4 minutes until the meat becomes somewhat elastic in consistency. I call this bouncy. This is the point when the fat becomes mixed with the protein in the pork, giving an even pink color and a more elastic texture. Look carefully for this change. If you take the mixing any farther than that, the stuffing will be too rubbery. Remove the meat from the mixer. Adjust the seasoning with salt and pepper.

Layout a wrapper and lay about 2-3 tablespoons of the filling in the center. Roll as for Spring Rolls (see page 36) and fry in 350° oil for 5-6 minutes. The rolls will be done when they turn golden brown and begin to pop up to the surface of the oil. Skim any foam that may rise to the top. Strain the oil into a clean receptacle and discard the solids. This may be made 2 days in advance. Imperial Rolls also freeze quite well.

INGREDIENTS

8 spring rolls wrappers, Thai style

6 ounces ground pork

1/2 medium carrot, peeled and cut into julienne

2 ounces angel-hair pasta, cooked

1/2 teaspoon chopped garlic

1/4 teaspoon chopped fresh ginger

1/2 teaspoon sambal (oriental chili paste)

1 tablespoon finely chopped scallions

1 teaspoon soy sauce

4 drops sesame oil

salt and freshly ground black pepper

1 egg

CRABCAKE *with Yellow Tomato Broth and Basil Mayonnaise*

My crabcakes are filled with jumbo lump crabmeat (and very little filler). And I strongly recommend you use crabmeat from the Gulf of Mexico. It absolutely rivals the very best crabmeat from the East including Chesapeake Bay. (Once you've prepared this recipe, you'll realize what a poor substitute most restaurants offer.)

TO MAKE THE YELLOW TOMATO BROTH
Place the yellow tomatoes in a blender and purée. Pass this mixture through a fine sieve using the back of a large spoon. Season with salt and pepper to taste. Stir in the extra virgin olive oil and chill.

TO MAKE THE SALAD GARNISH
Cut into the tomatoes into a julienne 1/8" wide. Toss with the basil, salt and pepper to taste. Toss again with the olive oil, chill and reserve. Garnish may be made up to one day in advance.

TO MAKE THE BASIL MAYONNAISE
Place the egg yolks, vinegar and mustard in the food processor fitted with a steel

MISE EN PLACE

Yellow Tomato Broth (recipe follows)

Salad Garnish (recipe follows)

Basil Mayonnaise (recipe follows)

Jumbo Lump Crabcake (recipe follows)

FOR THE SALAD GARNISH

2 ripe red tomatoes, peeled and seeded

4 leaves fresh basil, cut into a chiffonade (see Techniques Section)

1 teaspoon extra virgin olive oil

salt and pepper

FOR THE BROTH

2 ripe unpeeled yellow tomatoes

blade. Pulse the processor a few times to incorporate. With the machine running, slowly add the vegetable oil. The mayonnaise should be very thick. Add the parsley juice and pulse until incorporated. Transfer the mayonnaise to a container and stir in the basil chiffonade. Adjust taste with salt and pepper.

TO MAKE THE CRABCAKES

Preheat oven to 400°. Pick through the crabmeat to remove shells, leaving the large pieces of meat as intact as possible. Place the garlic, shallots, mustard, parsley and egg in a bowl and mix. Add the crabmeat and toss lightly. Add the breadcrumbs, again tossing lightly. Taste for salt and pepper.

Divide the crab mix into 4 equal portions and form each into the shape of a hockey puck. Refrigerate until ready to cook.

Heat the vegetable oil in an ovenproof sauté pan large enough to hold the crab cakes. When hot, place the crabcakes in the pan and sauté on each side over medium-high heat until golden brown, turning only once. These cakes are so big that they need to be finished in the oven so they will be warm throughout. Place the pan in the oven and bake for 5 minutes or until the crabcake is warmed throughout. Remove them from the oven and keep warm until ready to serve.

TO ASSEMBLE

Place the tomato salad garnish equally in each of 4 shallow serving bowls. Make sure the salad is larger than the crabcake so it will show through. Place the crabcake on top of the tomato salad. Put a dollop of the basil mayonnaise on top of the crabcake. Spoon the yellow tomato broth around the crabcake and serve.

1 teaspoon extra virgin olive oil

salt and pepper

FOR THE BASIL MAYONNAISE

2 egg yolks

1 tablespoon red wine vinegar

1 tablespoon Dijon mustard

1 cup vegetable oil

2 tablespoons green parsley juice
(see Techniques section)

10 basil leaves, cut into a fine chiffonade

salt and pepper

FOR THE JUMBO LUMP CRABCAKES

1 pound jumbo lump crabmeat

1 teaspoon chopped garlic

1 tablespoon finely minced shallots

1 tablespoon Dijon mustard

2 tablespoons chopped parsley

1 whole egg

2 ounces panko bread crumbs

2 tablespoons vegetable oil

salt and pepper to taste

OYSTERS *with Mignonette Sauce*

I abhor cocktail sauce; it masks the fresh flavor of the oyster. Mignonette is a perfect compliment to oysters with its peppery, tangy, fresh taste.

TO MAKE THE SAUCE

Combine the shallots, vinegar, black pepper and salt in a container and give it a good shake.

Open the oysters and cut through the muscle with a flexible paring knife or oyster knife, freeing the oyster. Cover a serving plate with a low mound of crushed ice. Nestle 6 oysters (resting in their shells) in the crushed ice. Spoon some of the mignonette sauce over the oysters and serve immediately.

MISE EN PLACE

24 fresh oysters such as Malpaque, Olympia, Kummomoto etc.

FOR THE MIGNONETTE SAUCE

2 medium shallots, cut into 1/8" dice

1/2 cup good red wine vinegar

2 tablespoons coarsely ground black pepper

kosher salt to taste

EDAMAME

Edamame are whole soybeans in the pod. I find them addictive. When I'm at Citizen I'm nibbling on them all night long. We serve these beans warm, sprinkled with kosher salt.

Fill a 1-gallon pot with cool water and bring to a boil. Place the edamame in the pot and boil for 2-3 minutes, or until the color of the beans turns bright green. Strain the edamame and sprinkle generously with the salt. Serve immediately. To serve cool, after draining, plunge the beans into ice water. Drain and sprinkle with salt.

INGREDIENTS

2 pounds edamame

1 1/2 teaspoons kosher salt

HIDDEN POACHED EGG
on Toasted Sourdough and Mustard Oil

I've de-constructed Eggs Benedict and put it back together with smoked salmon, a wonderful dijon mustard oil, and a grilled sourdough round (with applewood smoked bacon sprinkled around instead of Canadian bacon). Surprisingly light.

FOR THE POACHED EGGS

Bring 1 quart water and 1 cup white wine vinegar to a boil. Lower the heat to a simmer. Carefully break the eggs into the water and cook for 2 minutes each. Remove from the water and place in an ice bath to stop the cooking process. When the eggs have completely cooled, remove from the ice bath and cut off any dangly bits of the egg whites. The poached eggs maybe cooked one day in advance. To reheat, place in a quart of simmering water for 30 seconds and remove just as you are plating up.

FOR THE SOURDOUGH ROUNDS

Cut four slices of sourdough bread with a 3" cutter. Place the cut-out in an oven and lightly toast. Remove when browned.

Mix the olive oil and the lemon juice together and lightly toss with the mesclun greens. Reserve.

TO ASSEMBLE

Place a sourdough round in the center of a plate and place 1 ounce of the sliced smoked salmon over the round. Carefully place the poached egg on top of the salmon. Fold up the sides of the salmon to resemble a package. Drizzle the mustard oil around the plate and sprinkle the bacon over the top of the salmon and plate and garnish with a bit of the mesclun salad on the top of the salmon.

INGREDIENTS

6 ounces pre-sliced smoked salmon

4 soft poached eggs

4 grilled sourdough bread rounds

2 teaspoons mustard oil

1/8 cup diced Applewood bacon, cooked

1/8 cup extra virgin olive oil

juice of 1 lemon

FOR THE MUSTARD OIL

1/2 cup dijon mustard

2 tablespoons vegetable oil

Place both in a bowl, incorporate very well and reserve for later.

FOR THE MESCLUN SALAD

1 cup mesclun

1/8 cup extra virgin olive oil

juice of 1 lemon

SALADS

AN ENDANGERED SPECIES?

"This salad reminds me

never to overlook the real

essence of food,

to enjoy every bite and

remember the connection

between food and family."

I'm probably not the best person to ask about salads. That's because I became hooked on one type of dressing years ago – Roquefort – and nothing else quite satisfies my palate. In fact, I could eat chunks of Roquefort cheese all day long, like popcorn. Roquefort is one of those foods that remind me of why I love cooking so much. Its pungent smell takes me back to my childhood and the first time I had the nerve to try eating it. Its story – how it has been produced in the same way, in the same place in France for hundreds of years – reminds me that as a chef, I am part of an enduring tradition. Plus, few people may know that this is a cheese made from sheep's milk. (I'm sure there are those who would never eat anything as exotic as 'sheep's milk cheese' who love Roquefort.) This is proof that there is a wide variety of 'different' foods to be savored, if only people would be open to the experience.

In certain parts of the country, salads are disappearing from menus. In Dallas restaurants, however, people expect to see an array of salads. From my Phyllo-encased Caesar Salad to Heirloom Tomato Salad with Sherry Basil Vinaigrette, the presentation and ingredient possiblities are endless. A few of these salads can be served as entrées such as Cobb Salad with Grilled Chicken Breast and Assorted Oils, Seared Rare Tuna with Three Peppers, or Kalamata Bread Salad.

When I look at the salad recipes I've included in this book, I'm still drawn to the most simple one – the wedge of romaine with creamy Roquefort and cracked pepper. As I said, I'm more than a little partial to Roquefort, but this recipe is more than just a salad. It's a time machine that takes me back to when I was a teenager learning to appreciate both the role of strong flavors and the idea that simple recipes can sometimes be the best. This salad reminds me never to overlook the real essence of food, to enjoy every bite and remember the connection between food and family.

Not everyone knows this, but the Cobb has a star-studded past. It was first served years ago at the then famous Brown Derby in Hollywood. My version creates a ring of salad topped with chicken placed tepee style. It's my best selling salad (hats off to The Brown Derby).

TO MAKE THE VINAIGRETTE

Whisk the vinegar, egg yolk and mustard together in a bowl. Slowly whisk in the oil to emulsify. Season with salt and pepper to taste. Refrigerate.

TO MAKE THE SALAD

In a large bowl, toss the avocado, hard-boiled eggs, tomato, bacon, blue cheese, lettuce and enough champagne vinaigrette to just moisten the salad. With a spoon, mash the salad until it resembles a loose guacamole. Season with salt and pepper to taste. Cover the surface with plastic wrap and reserve.

TO MAKE THE CHICKEN BREASTS

Grill the chicken breast until just done, about 5 minutes per side. Reserve and keep warm.

ASSEMBLY

In the middle of 4 plates, use the 4" ring and place equal amounts of the Cobb salad inside the ring. With moderate pressure, press the salad down with a spoon or fork until it is flush with the top of the 4" ring. Refrigerate the salad for 1 hour. Using one hand, hold down the top of the molded salad while you remove the ring, giving it a slight twist as you lift up if it doesn't move easily. Slice the warm chicken and place on top of the salad in a grid fashion: two one way, then two the other and so on. Drizzle the plate with the oils and serve immediately.

INGREDIENTS

2 ripe avocados, peeled, seeded and broken into large pieces

2 hard-boiled eggs, peeled and grated

1 ripe tomato, peeled, seeded and diced

4 pieces diced and cooked bacon

6 ounces blue cheese, preferably Roquefort

1 head romaine lettuce, cut into a julienne or a rough chiffonade

1 cup Champagne Vinaigrette (recipe follows)

4 boneless chicken breasts, around 6 ounces each

Salt and freshly ground black pepper

1 tablespoon basil oil (optional)

1 tablespoon chili oil (optional)

SPECIAL EQUIPMENT

4 - 4" rings, approximately 2" high

FOR THE CHAMPAGNE VINAIGRETTE

1/4 cup champagne vinegar

1 egg yolk

2 teaspoons Dijon mustard

2/3 cup canola oil

Salt and freshly ground black pepper

KALAMATA BREAD SALAD

My version – and an unusual one at that – of a greek salad with many different mediterranean tastes. The bread in the salad provides the crunch (replacing the crouton).

Place the 12 slices of thinly cut Kalamata bread on a sheet pan and brush with oil. Bake in a 350° oven for 8-10 minutes or until lightly browned. Remove from the oven and place in an airtight container until ready to use.

In a large non-reactive bowl place the mesclun artichoke hearts, Kalamata olives, tomato, feta cheese and mozzarella cheese. Pour the champagne vinaigrette over salad ingredients and gently toss. Season with salt and pepper.

ASSEMBLY
Place a slice of browned Kalamata bread on a plate. Place salad mix on top of the bread slice. Repeat procedure 2 or more times and serve.

INGREDIENTS

12 paper thin slices Kalamata bread (sourdough may be substituted)

6 cups loosely packed mesclun

1/2 cup champagne vinaigrette (see page 49)

1/2 cup artichoke hearts, preferably fresh, sliced or quartered

1/4 cup pitted Kalamata olives

1/4 cup julienne tomato concassé

1/4 cup feta cheese

1/4 cup fresh mozzarella

1/2 cup extra virgin olive oil

Salt and pepper

MY MOM'S WEDGE OF ROMAINE

When you've eaten a salad your entire life, it becomes comfort food. My mother's version used iceberg lettuce but that's one of the only differences. This is on The Mercury's menu.

TO MAKE THE DRESSING
Place egg yolks, vinegar and Dijon mustard in food processor fitted with a steel blade. While the motor is running, slowly add the vegetable oil to emulsify the mixture. Remove the mayonnaise to a clean bowl. Place the Roquefort and cold water in a small bowl and mix together until it resembles a paste. Scrape the paste into the mayonnaise and mix well. Refrigerate.

ASSEMBLY
Cut the romaine lettuce in half lengthwise then in half again. Place one wedge on a plate then cross the other romaine wedge over the other half on the plate. Spoon a generous amount of the Roquefort dressing on top of the romaine; sprinkle with Roquefort cheese around and or on the salad. Sprinkle the salad with the tomato julienne and cracked black pepper.

MISE EN PLACE

2 heads of romaine lettuce, blemished outside leaves removed, soaked in cold water and drained

2 cups Roquefort Dressing (recipe follows)

1 cup extra Roquefort cheese, crumbled

1/4 cup tomato concassé, cut into julienne

1 tablespoon freshly cracked black pepper

FOR THE ROQUEFORT DRESSING

3 egg yolks

1 tablespoon good red wine vinegar

1 1/2 tablespoons Dijon mustard

1 1/2 cups vegetable oil

8 ounces Roquefort cheese

2 ounces cold water

HEIRLOOM TOMATO SALAD *with Sherry Basil Vinaigrette*

For me, summer means one thing – heirloom tomatoes are in season. These tomatoes are incomparable in flavor and succulence (they are the genetic source for all other tomatoes). With a little salt and pepper, I can eat one like an apple. Make it a point to find these.

TO TOAST THE WALNUTS

Place the walnuts and pecans on a cookie sheet and bake at 350° for 8-10 minutes until slightly roasted. When done, slide onto a plate to stop the cooking, sprinkle with salt and reserve in an airtight container.

TO MAKE THE FAVA BEANS

Remove the favas from their pods while bringing 1 pint of water to a boil. Add the beans to the boiling water and cook for 10 seconds. Remove from the boiling water and plunge the beans into cold ice water. Remove from the water and carefully peel the outer shell covering the inner pea. Discard the shells. Reserve in a cool place.

FOR THE SALAD ASSEMBLY

Cut and or slice the tomatoes into different shapes and sizes. If you have small cherry tomatoes leave them whole. Place the larger tomato pieces on the bottom of the plates. Then build up a small mountain with the rest of the tomatoes. Intermittently place slices of julienned red onion around the tomato mound. Drizzles the sherry basil vinaigrette around the tomato, sprinkle with extra basil and toasted walnuts. Garnish with strips of asiago cheese and freshly cracked pepper.

MISE EN PLACE

Sherry Basil Vinaigrette (recipe follows)

1 ounce toasted walnuts

1 ounce toasted pecans

2 pounds fresh fava beans

1 1/2 pounds assorted heirloom tomatoes

1/2 small red onion, cut into a fine julienne

12 strips shaved asiago cheese

Cracked black pepper

SHERRY BASIL VINAIGRETTE

1/2 cup extra virgin olive oil

1/8 cup Sherry vinegar

1/2 teaspoon finely chopped shallots

8 basil leaves, cut into a chiffonade

Salt and freshly ground black pepper

I love tweaking classic recipes. In this case, the romaine leaves are completely wrapped in phyllo creating a salad 'burrito.' This is then baked (the outside becomes crisp – which substitutes for the crouton – while the leaves inside stay cool).

TO PREPARE THE DRESSING

Place the mustard, egg yolks, garlic, vinegar, and Worcestershire in a blender and purée until smooth. Place the purée in a bowl and slowly add the oils to emulsify. Add the lemon juice and season with salt and pepper.

TO PREPARE THE PHYLLO

Follow the box directions on how to defrost and keep fresh. Lay 1 sheet of the phyllo out on a clean work surface brushed with oil. Then sprinkle the parmesan cheese on top, place another sheet over the cheese; brush with olive oil and sprinkle the chives on top. Place another sheet over the chives and brush with olive oil and sprinkle with freshly cracked black pepper; place another sheet over the pepper.

TO PREPARE THE ROMAINE LETTUCE

Remove the romaine leaves from their stem and place in a bowl. Sprinkle with parmesan cheese and toss the leaves with the Caesar dressing.

TO ASSEMBLE

Place equal amounts of the tossed romaine lettuce on an angle on top of the phyllo dough; fold up the edges and roll up the lettuce. It should resemble a burrito in shape.

TO BAKE

Place the phyllo Caesar on a sheet pan and cook for 3-4 minutes in a 500° oven. Bake until the rolls are lightly browned. Remove the phyllo Caesar from the oven and slice on a bias. Drizzle with the remaining Caesar dressing and sprinkle the shaved asiago around the lettuce.

MISE EN PLACE

2 heads of romaine lettuce

16 sheets of Phyllo dough

1 cup Parmigiano-Reggiano cheese

2 cups Caesar Dressing (recipe follows)

2 tablespoons freshly cracked black pepper

2 tablespoons finely diced chives

1/2 cup extra virgin olive oil

1/2 cup asiago cheese, shaved

FOR THE CAESAR DRESSING

1 cup extra virgin olive oil

1 cup vegetable oil

2 egg yolks

1 tablespoon Dijon mustard

4 cloves peeled garlic

1 teaspoon Worcestershire sauce

2 tablespoons red wine vinegar

Juice of 2 lemons

Salt and freshly ground black pepper

SEARED RARE TUNA *with Three Pepper, Cannellini Bean and Kalamata Salad*

This dish works as a salad, an appetizer or an entree (it's that versatile). The cool, rare tuna on top of a pungent picante-style three pepper and bean 'relish' is a truly wonderful way to enjoy tuna and summer.

TO MAKE THE TUNA

Salt and pepper the tuna pieces. In a very hot pan, lightly sear (20 seconds) the tuna on both sides. Remove from the pan. Allow the tuna to rest for 5 minutes. It should resemble a very rare steak in appearance.

Meanwhile, place the beans, peppers, tomato, olives, scallions, basil, shallots, garlic, vinegar and olive oil in a large bowl. Toss to combine.

Place the peppers and bean relish equally in the middle of the 4 plates.
Slice the tuna 1/4" thick and place on top of the relish. Drizzle with white truffle oil (optional) and garnish with a nice basil sprig. Serve immediately.

MISE EN PLACE

4, 4 ounces each portions of sushi quality tuna

1/2 cup cooked cannellini beans

1/8 cup diced red bell pepper

1/8 cup diced yellow bell pepper

1/8 cup diced green bell pepper

1 tomato, peeled, seeded and diced

2 tablespoons kalamata olives, sliced

1 scallion finely sliced

10 fresh picked basil leaves

1 teaspoon diced shallots

1/2 teaspoon chopped garlic

1/8 cup balsamic vinegar

1/2 cup extra virgin olive oil

white truffle oil (optional)

The soba noodle is a buckwheat noodle. Here I toss the noodle in a vinaigrette and add a three pepper relish and jalapeño. (I think you will enjoy making this oriental vinaigrette. It has a distinctive flavor.)

TO MAKE THE NOODLES

Bring 2 quarts of water to a rapid boil, add the package of noodles and cook until al dente, about 4 minutes. Strain and run under cold water, toss the chilled pasta with 2 tablespoons vegetable oil to prevent sticking. Toss all the peppers, ginger and scallions together in a bowl. Add the soba noodles, toss with enough of the oriental vinaigrette to moisten.

TO MAKE THE VINAIGRETTE

Whisk the garlic, sugar, vinegar, soy sauce, sesame oil and vegetable oil together. Reserve.

ASSEMBLY

Place a shiso leaf in the middle of each plate, place equal amounts of pasta to one side of the shiso leaf. Sprinkle with toasted peanuts and serve.

MISE EN PLACE

1 (12.7ounce) package soba noodles

1 cup Oriental Vinaigrette (recipe follows)

1/4 cup toasted chopped peanuts

4 shiso leaves, available at Japanese markets

4 sprigs fresh mint

8 ounces Pepper Relish (recipe follows)

FOR THE VINAIGRETTE

1 teaspoon minced garlic

3/4 cup sugar

1/2 cup rice wine vinegar

2 tablespoons soy sauce

1/2 teaspoons sesame oil

1 cup vegetable oil

FOR THE PEPPER RELISH

1 medium red bell pepper

1 medium yellow bell pepper

1 medium green bell pepper

1 jalapeño chile, seeded and cut in a brunoise

1/2 teaspoon grated ginger

2 scallions, finely sliced

TOMATO & SMALL MOZZARELLA SALAD

TO PREPARE THE TOMATO

Remove the stem scar from each tomato with a paring knife; mark an "x" on the bottom of the tomato and plunge them into a pot of boiling water for 5-10 seconds or until the skin begins to peel back. Immediately plunge the tomatoes in ice water. Carefully peel the tomato skin. Slice the top of the tomato off, cutting a hole through where you trimmed the stem scar and reserve. Carefully scoop most of the meat from the inside of the tomatoes. Try to remove as many of the seeds as possible while leaving the body of the tomato intact. Season the inside of the tomato with salt and pepper and chill.

TO ASSEMBLE

Season the mozzarella balls with salt and pepper. Place the 3 mozzarella balls into the cavity of the tomatoes. Drizzle half of the pesto over the mozzarella balls. Make 2 small bundles of lettuce (to resemble a bouquet) and place the bouquet through the stem/core part of the tomato top to hold them securely. Drizzle the plate with extra virgin olive oil, the balsamic vinegar and the remaining basil pesto. Place the asiago strips randomly around the tomato and serve.

MISE EN PLACE

2 very ripe red tomatoes

6 fresh bocconcini (small mozzarella balls about 1-1/2" in diameter)

2 tablespoons Basil Pesto (see page 28)

4 tablespoons good quality extra virgin olive oil

balsamic vinegar

asiago cheese shavings

1 cup mesclun

salt and freshly ground black pepper

While this salad takes a bit of preparation, it pays off in taste and appearance. It really is a summer show stopper.

TO PREPARE AND COOK ARTICHOKES

With a small knife cut the leaves from around each artichoke using a circular motion until you reach the tender inner leaves. Cut off the leaves and continue to trim the artichoke hearts down to the base, removing all the tough fibrous outer skin. Rub the hearts all over with the cut lemon.

In a medium saucepan bring 1 1/2 quarts of water to a boil with 2 tablespoons of the lemon juice and 1 teaspoon salt. Add two of the artichoke hearts and boil until tender, about 30 minutes. Drain and let cool. Scoop out the hairy chokes with a spoon. Cut the artichokes hearts in small wedges and set aside in a bowl.

Meanwhile in a large saucepan or deep fryer heat the vegetable oil to 350°. Scoop out the chokes of the 2 remaining uncooked artichoke hearts. Using a sharp knife slice the hearts crosswise as thin as possible. Working in three batches fry the artichoke slices until golden (2-3 minutes). Transfer with a slotted spoon to paper towels to drain. Sprinkle lightly with salt.

Bring a large saucepan of salted water to a boil. Add the green beans and cook until tender, 3-5 minutes. Using a wire skimmer, transfer the beans to a colander and refresh under cold running water. Drain again, pat dry and add to the bowl with the artichoke wedges. Repeat this process with the waxed beans.

Return the water in the saucepan to a boil. Add the asparagus pieces and cook until tender 3-5 minutes. Using a wire skimmer, transfer the beans to a colander and refresh under cold running water. Drain again; pat dry and add to the bowl with the artichoke wedges.

ASSEMBLY

Arrange the tomato slices on four plates. Sprinkle the shallots, 1 tablespoon of the lemon juice and 2 tablespoons of the olive oil on top. Sprinkle lightly with salt and pepper. In a bowl, toss the mesclun with the chives and chervil. Add 2 tablespoons of the olive oil and 1 tablespoon of the lemon juice, season with salt and pepper and toss well. Mound the salad greens on the tomatoes. Season the cooked vegetables with 2 tablespoons of the olive oil, 1 teaspoon of the lemon juice, salt and pepper. Garnish each salad with the mushrooms and artichoke chips.

INGREDIENTS

4 large artichokes

1 lemon halved

1/4 cup plus 2 teaspoons fresh lemon juice

salt

3 cups vegetable oil for frying

1/4 pound very thin green beans trimmed

1/4 pound waxed beans

8 asparagus spears tender tip portion only, cut in 1" lengths

2 medium tomatoes (about 1.5 pounds) peeled and very thinly sliced

1 tablespoon minced shallot

6 tablespoons plus 2 teaspoons extra virgin olive oil

Freshly ground pepper

1/2 pound mesclun or young mixed greens such as mache, young chicory, oak leaf lettuce and arugula

2 tablespoons finely minced chives

2 tablespoons coarsely chopped chervil

4 fresh mushrooms thinly sliced

SOUPS

"While the recipes have exact measurements, soup recipes let you have more leeway and flexibility than other recipes. If you're concerned that a soup is too thick or too thin, don't worry. It's soup."

Soups obviously have a cold weather reputation. And for good reason. There's something about freezing weather and a bowl of hot soup that go together. But I think we can also agree, the right soup can be perfect any time of year. So to make it easy for you to 'think soup' more often, I've made it, well, easy for you. A blender is the only apparatus you'll need to make any of my soups. And while the recipes have exact measurements, soup recipes let you have more leeway and flexibility than other recipes. If you're concerned that a soup is too thick or too thin, don't worry. It's soup. In fact, I've included one recipe that takes me out on a real limb regarding what ingredients to use. It's called Garbage soup. (Like a lot of things, it sounds better in French). Garbage soup depends on you, not me. I show you how to go through your pantry and refrigerator and mix what you have on hand into a surprisingly tasty cream soup.

Almost all of my soups, with some exception, are spicy soups. In Texas, we eat spicy Tex-Mex food year round, so 'hot' soup is expected. If you're not sure how spicy you like your soup, start with the cream of poblano and add the pico de gallo to taste.

I'm not much of a fan of fruit soups. But for those of you looking for a warm weather or summer soup, I have included my chilled 'gazpacho style' charred yellow tomato soup. This is my variation of a classic and I think it needs to be in your repertoire.

I love all the soups in this chapter, but one soup I want to draw to your attention to is my Shiner Bock Sharp Cheddar soup. Besides being a great soup made with sharp cheddar cheese and dark ale, the recipe also calls for rustic croutons to be added as a final touch. I have an affinity for good croutons. I can be seen nibbling fresh ones all day long. While my favorite crouton for this soup is bacon basil, trust your own palate and feel free to create any number of different flavored croutons.

YELLOW TOMATO GAZPACHO
with Poblano Hush Puppies

My version of gazpacho. The first difference is yellow tomatoes vs. red tomatoes. The real difference, however, is that you purée only the tomatoes, not all of the ingredients. And for an interesting temperature contrast, I've added a southern treat of fried cornmeal fritters, aka, hush puppies.

Place the yellow tomato halves, sliced onion, garlic and whole jalapeños under a hot broiler until they are charred and softened. Remove and place ingredients in a ricer. If you do not have a ricer, place the tomatoes, jalapeños, onions, garlic and 1/2 of the seeded cucumbers in a blender and pulse. Do not over-purée, it should be slightly chunky. Add the rest of the diced cucumber, tomato concassé, and peppers. Season with salt and pepper to taste. Garnish with fresh cilantro. Chill.

Blister the poblano under a broiler or over an open flame. Wrap the pepper in plastic for 20 minutes. Remove the plastic wrap and peel the poblano pepper. Dice into 1/4"pieces and reserve.

Mix the flour, cornmeal, baking powder, scallions, cayenne, sugar, salt and pepper to taste in a bowl and add the diced roasted poblano. Whisk the eggs, oil and milk together in a bowl and combine with the dry ingredients. Preheat a fryer to 350°. Using a tablespoon, slide a dollop of hush puppy mixture into the oil. Turn the hush puppies over in the oil to fry evenly; when they begin to float they should be done. Remove and drain on a paper towel.

Ladle the soup into bowls. Place a couple of the warm Poblano hush puppies on top of the chilled soup and serve.

INGREDIENTS

6 yellow tomatoes, stem scar removed and halved

1 medium red onion, peeled and sliced

2 cloves of garlic, peeled

2 whole jalapeño chiles

1 English cucumber, peeled, seeded and cut into 1/2" dice

1 red bell pepper, seeded and diced

1 poblano chile pepper, seeded and diced

1 green bell pepper, seeded and diced

2 tablespoons tomato concassé

FOR THE POBLANO HUSH PUPPIES

1 poblano chile pepper, blistered, peeled and diced

1/2 cup flour

1/2 cup cornmeal

2 tablespoons baking powder

1/2 cup milk

2 eggs

1 tablespoon oil

2 scallions, diced

1 pinch cayenne

1/2 teaspoon sugar

salt and freshly ground black pepper

2 quarts vegetable oil for frying

CHOCOLATE BLACK BEAN SOUP

Makes 2 quarts

The Mexican-influenced cooking in Texas has always included a mysterious, dark sauce called molé. Chocolate is one of its ingredients. With that in mind, I've created a soup that contains cocoa powder. It adds that depth of flavor that transforms this from being just bean soup into something special. Don't be afraid to add the cinnamon...it goes well with the cocoa. I can say this in all honesty – it's one of my favorite soups.

Warm the oil in a 1-gallon saucepan and add the black beans and bacon, cooking until the bacon begins to crisp. Add the onion, celery, bell pepper, garlic and jalapeños. Sauté until the vegetables are softened. Pour the vegetable stock over all and bring to a simmer for 1 hour or until the black beans are tender. Add the cilantro and continue to cook for five more minutes. Add the cinnamon and the cocoa powder. Pour the soup into the blender and purée until smooth, pass through a chinois or fine strainer – adjust the seasoning to taste and serve. We typically garnish the soup with Pico de Gallo (see page 64), fried tortillas and/or cheddar cheese.

INGREDIENTS

3 cups dried black beans, rinsed and soaked in water overnight

1 tablespoon vegetable oil

4 ounces applewood smoked bacon, chopped

1 medium yellow onion, roughly chopped

2 ribs celery, roughly chopped

1 green bell pepper, seeded and roughly chopped

4 cloves of garlic, peeled

2 jalapeños, seeded and roughly chopped

3 quarts Vegetable Stock (see Basics)

1 bunch cilantro, trimmed and roughly chopped

1/2 teaspoon cinnamon

1 1/2 tablespoons cocoa powder

2 bay leaves

salt and freshly ground black pepper

GARBAGE SOUP

Makes 2 quarts

This isn't shock value. This is meant to inspire you to create great soup from any and all vegetables in your pantry or refrigerator. (Actually this is a classic French soup – Garbure – which sounds so much more refined in French.)

Place the butter in a heavy gauge soup pot over medium high heat and when it begins to brown add the onion, celery, carrot, potato, turnip, pepper, zucchini, squash and garlic. Sauté for 10 minutes. Add the vegetable stock and the herbs. Bring to a simmer and cook until the vegetables are soft. Place the soup in a blender and puree until smooth, pass the soup through a chinois or a fine strainer. Add the cream, celery salt and taste for salt and pepper. Chill. This soup can be made 3 days in advance.

INGREDIENTS

2 tablespoons unsalted butter

1 medium onion, peeled and roughly cut

2 ribs of celery, roughly cut

1 jumbo carrot, peeled and roughly cut

1 Idaho potato, peeled and roughly cut

1 medium turnip, peeled and roughly cut

1/2 red bell pepper, seeded and roughly cut

1 small zucchini, roughly cut

1 small yellow squash, roughly cut

2 cloves garlic

2 1/2 quarts Vegetable Stock (see Basics)

1 sprig fresh thyme

1 bay leaf

2 cups heavy cream

1/2 tablespoon celery salt

salt and freshly ground black pepper

CANNELLINI BEAN AND ESCAROLE SOUP

Makes 2 quarts

This rustic Tuscan Italian soup is the quintessential full-bodied, full-flavored soup, but requires only a few ingredients. It fits with my theory: there is no connection between the number of ingredients and the quality of any soup.

TO MAKE THE SOUP

In a large stockpot heat the 2 tablespoons vegetable oil. Add the sliced applewood bacon and cook until barely crisp. Add all the vegetables including the cannellini beans. Cook for 5 minutes, then add vegetable stock and bay leaves. Bring to a boil and simmer for 45 minutes or until the cannellini beans are tender. Remove half of the soup and puree it lightly. Return the puree to rest of the soup. Season to taste and keep warm.

TO MAKE THE ESCAROLE

Tear the leaves from the escarole. Smoke the oil in a large sauté pan and add the escarole, sautéing on very high heat for 1 minute. Add 1 teaspoon chopped garlic to the pan and sauté for 30 more seconds. Season with salt, pepper and add to the soup. Season to taste.

Spoon the soup into bowls and garnish with large rustic croutons.

INGREDIENTS

2 cups cannellini beans – soaked in water overnight

1 medium onion, cut into small dice

2 ribs celery, cut into small dice

2 cloves garlic, finely chopped

Sautéed Escarole (recipe follows)

2 quarts Vegetable Stock (see Basics)

1/4 cup diced applewood smoked bacon

2 bay leaves

2 tablespoons vegetable oil

salt and pepper

FOR THE ESCAROLE

1 head escarole, cleaned, rinsed thoroughly and patted dry

1 teaspoon olive oil

1 teaspoon chopped garlic

salt and freshly ground black pepper

CHEDDAR CHEESE SHINER BOCK SOUP

Makes 2 quarts

If you're not from Texas, you might not know that Shiner Bock is a medium-dark, malty, local beer. Substitute freely, but try not to use 'regular' beer. (I use Heineken when I'm making this at home.) This soup should turn out velvety smooth.

Heat the butter in a heavy gauge soup pot, when it begins to brown add the onion, peppers, garlic, celery and jalapeños. Sweat the vegetables for 10-15 minutes and stir in flour, mixing thoroughly. Immediately add the chicken stock. Continue stirring so the vegetables do not settle to the bottom and burn. Add the beer and simmer the soup for 30 minutes. Add the cheese, stirring well and cook for 5 more minutes. Remove from the stove, pour into blender with motor running and purée. Pass through a fine strainer. Return the strained soup to the stove and add the cream and heat through. Adjust the seasoning with salt and pepper. Pour the soup into a bowl and sprinkle with the bacon. Spread a bread round with basil pesto and float on the soup. Sprinkle cheese around the pesto round and serve.

INGREDIENTS

8 ounces unsalted butter

1 medium yellow onion, peeled and roughly chopped

2 green bell peppers, seeded and roughly chopped

1 yellow bell peppers, seeded and roughly chopped

3 cloves garlic, roughly chopped

2 ribs celery, roughly chopped

2 jalapeño chile peppers, seeded and chopped

1 cup all purpose flour

1 quart chicken stock

1 bottle of Shiner Bock beer

1 3/4 cups grated extra sharp cheddar cheese

1 cup heavy cream

4 toasted bread rounds

2 tablespoons basil pesto

1/4 cup of cooked slab bacon cut into a 1/4" dice

salt and freshly ground black pepper

CREAMED POBLANO SOUP *with Pico de Gallo*

This soup gives you a taste of the Southwest without the intense peppery heat. Poblano peppers generally produce a mild, flavorful soup with a wonderful green color (don't forget to add the cilantro or spinach before you purée). The pico de gallo adds interesting color and turns up the heat.

Toss ingredients for Pico de Gallo together.

Place the butter in a heated large heavy gauge soup pot and when it begins to brown add the onion, celery, poblanos, jalapeños and garlic, sautéing 5-6 minutes. Slowly stir in the flour and mix well. Add the vegetable stock, bring to a simmer and cook 30 minutes. Add the cilantro and spinach and heat through. Pour the soup into a blender and purée. Pass through a fine strainer, and pour into bowls. Garnish with a spoonful of Pico de Gallo.

INGREDIENTS

3 tablespoons butter

1 medium yellow onion, peeled and roughly cut

2 ribs celery, roughly cut

4 poblano peppers, blistered, peeled, seeded and diced

2 jalapeños chiles, seeded and diced

2 quarts Vegetable Stock (see Basics)

2 cloves garlic

1/3 cup flour

2 bunches of cilantro

1 cup loosely packed fresh spinach

Pico de Gallo (recipe below)

PICO DE GALLO

6 ripe tomatoes, cut into a concassé

1/4 medium red onion, finely diced

3 jalapeño chiles, seeded and finely diced

1/4 cup loosely packed cilantro leaves

Juice of 3 limes

salt and freshly ground black pepper

1 tablespoon vegetable oil

CAMEMBERT CHEESE SOUP

This recipe is an homage to my first job and my first real chef/mentor, Jean Lafont, who always had a Brie soup on his menu. Thanks, Jean, for both the encouragement and for being such an unrelenting taskmaster.

Add the unsalted butter to a heated large heavy soup pot. When the butter begins to brown, add the mushrooms, leeks and sauté until soft. Add the chicken stock and bring to a simmer. Cook for 1 hour and then add 1/2 of the cheese, all the scallions and cook for 5 minutes or until the cheese has melted. Mix the Marsala and cornstarch together and add to the soup to thicken. Simmer for 5 minutes. Strain the soup through a fine sieve and stir in the cream. Season to taste with salt and pepper. You should have smooth, velvety cream soup. Slice the remaining Camembert and place on the toasted bread rounds. Pour the soup into ovenproof bowls and float a Camembert crouton on top of the soup. Put the bowls under a broiler to lightly brown, about 2-3 minutes. Remove from broiler, sprinkle chives around the crouton on the soup and serve.

INGREDIENTS

2 tablespoons unsalted butter

1 cup sliced mushrooms

2 leeks, white part only, cleaned and thinly sliced

26 ounces chicken stock

8 ounces Camembert cheese, rind removed and cubed

2 bunch scallions, thinly sliced

1 cup Marsala wine

3 ounces cornstarch

8 ounces heavy cream

salt and freshly ground black pepper

4 slices of round bread for croutons

1 tablespoon finely chopped chives

My tortilla soup would be classified as 'peasant style', that is, with clear broth where you can see the individual ingredients. A simple soup with authentic Mexican flavor and panache.

Heat the stock in a 4-quart soup pot. Place the chicken in the stock and bring to a simmer. Cook for about 30 minutes or until tender. Skim the fat that accumulates on the surface. Remove the chicken from the stock and add all of the peppers and onions to the pot. Cook for 15 minutes. Continue to remove the fat from the surface of the stock, skim – skim – skim. Pull the meat from the cooked chicken into rustic, bite-size pieces and return to the simmering pot. Add the peas, diced tomatoes, cilantro and cumin. Season with salt and pepper to taste.

Pour the soup into bowls and garnish with grated Monterey jack cheese, diced avocados, julienned strips of fried tortillas and wedges of lime.

INGREDIENTS

1 quart Brown Chicken Stock (see Basics)

1 whole chicken

1 red bell pepper, seeded and diced

1 green bell pepper, seeded and diced

1 Poblano pepper, seeded and diced

1 red onion, diced

4 tomatoes, peeled and diced

1 cup shelled fresh English peas

1/2 cup diced tomatoes

1/2 cup cilantro leaves, loosely packed

1 teaspoon cumin

salt and freshly ground black pepper

F O W L

"Red meat birds – duck,

dove, pigeon – can be

cooked as if you were

cooking a steak: rare,

medium rare, etc."

Here's something you may not know, but the best way to think about cooking fowl is to first classify the bird you're cooking as either white meat or red meat. Chicken, turkey and quail are 'white' meat. Birds that walk on the ground are considered white meat, ostrich being the exception. Duck, dove and pigeon (which is really just an oversized dove), are 'red' meat – these birds all fly.

Here's the important distinction. White meat birds need to cook all the way through. Red meat birds can be cooked as if you were cooking steak, that is: rare, medium rare, etc. Hopefully, this should give you confidence when you tackle the duck recipes. (As a note, the duck you buy in the grocery store is all pen-raised and has a wonderful mild flavor).

Quail is a Texas favorite, but too many hunters make this same mistake: they clean the quail in the field and when removing the feathers, take the skin off the breast as well. While it is much harder work to remove the feathers without removing the skin, give it a try. Grilling quail with the skin on locks in the juices and flavors. The difference will astound you.

The remaining recipes feature chicken. And while I do believe chicken is overused, I'd like to make a proud confession. My last meal on earth would be fried chicken, black-eyed peas, turnip greens, mashed potatoes and iced tea. While this may convince you that I am just a Southern boy at heart, I would rather convince you to go to the trouble of making my fried chicken. Don't let the three day marinade part scare you away. Some things are worth the effort. One last word about chicken. When you're looking at chicken in the market, don't be concerned if you see the bird has yellow fat. In fact, that's what you should look for – it's an indication of how much corn is in the diet (yellow fat is present in even free-range chicken).

As much as I love chicken (especially fried), there is so much more in the world of fowl. I hope these recipes tempt you to go exploring.

GRILLED QUAIL *in an Herbed Popover with Applewood Bacon and Chanterelle Braise*

Years ago (as out of date as this may sound) prime rib was considered fine dining, and it was always served with a popover (or Yorkshire pudding). I loved the idea of updating the popover. The result: an herbed popover stuffed with quail and surrounded by sauce. It actually comes together in a spectacular way.

FOR THE POPOVERS

Preheat oven to 350°. Whisk the eggs together thoroughly in a glass or stainless steel bowl. Whisk in the flour, then lightly whisk in the milk, duck fat, thyme, salt and pepper. Strain. Lay a piece of plastic wrap on the surface of the batter and allow the mixture to reach room temperature.

Place a muffin pan in the preheated oven. When the pan is hot, spray every other compartment with non-stick spray. Pour the batter into the sprayed compartments, filling just short of the edges. Bake the popovers for 30-35 minutes or until they are fully risen and dry. Remove from the oven and keep in a warm place.

FOR THE QUAIL

Preheat the grill until it is very hot. Season the quail with salt and pepper. Brush them with olive oil and grill for 4 minutes on each side. The quail meat should be slightly pink. Reserve in a warm spot.

FOR THE SAUCE

Heat the vegetable oil in a sauté pan over high heat. When the oil is smoking, add the chanterelles and sauté for 2 minutes. Season with salt and pepper and add the shallots, cooking for 20 seconds more. Add the vermouth and reduce by two thirds, scraping all the bits from the bottom of the pan. Add the demi-glace and cook until the desired consistency is reached. Add the cooked bacon. Season with salt and pepper.

ASSEMBLY

Place one warm popover in the middle of a plate. Poke a hole in the top of the popover and place the quail in the popover. The legs should be sticking upward. Spoon half of the sauce inside the popover and over the quail. Drizzle the other half around the plate. Take a little bunch of mesclun mix, gather them at the stem ends and form the greens into a bouquet. Tuck it inside the popover. Serve immediately.

INGREDIENTS

4 whole eggs

16 ounces all-purpose flour

1 pint whole milk

1 ounce duck fat, melted (optional)

1/2 teaspoon chopped fresh thyme

4 semi-boneless quail

extra virgin olive oil

1 tablespoon vegetable oil

2 ounces fresh golden chanterelles

2 tablespoons diced shallots

3 ounces dry vermouth

1 cup demi-glace

2 ounces diced applewood bacon, cooked crisp

1 loose cup mesclun

salt and freshly ground black pepper

CHINESE LACQUERED DUCK *with Coffee Mandarin Glaze*

Served at my asian restaurant, Citizen; the lacquered color (almost black) comes from the coffee glaze and the honey. The result is duck with a sweet, molasses flavor that can be enjoyed as part of a noodle salad or as an entree by itself.

TO MAKE CHINESE LACQUERED DUCK

Rub ducks thoroughly with salt. Place the ducks on a rack set over a shallow pan and refrigerate uncovered for 24 hours. Rinse the ducks well under cold running water to remove salt. Cut off any excess fat and discard.

Preheat the oven to 450°. In a stockpot, bring 1 gallon of water to a boil over high heat; stir in the honey. Immerse 1 of the ducks in the boiling honey water for 4 minutes. Carefully remove the duck from the water and drain well. Repeat with the second duck. Set the ducks on a wire rack in a roasting pan. Roast ducks for 30 minutes; reduce oven temperature to 300° and roast for about an hour longer, until the skin resembles black lacquer.

Meanwhile, in a heavy, medium sized non-reactive saucepan, cook the sugar over moderate heat stirring until it becomes a light brown caramel. Immediately stir in the butter. When it has melted stir in the orange juice, optional coffee and coffee liqueur. Simmer until the sugar dissolves completely then stir in the cornstarch and simmer until thickened, about 3 minutes. Remove from heat and keep warm

To carve the ducks, remove the breast and legs from the carcasses leaving the skin intact. Slice the leg meat off the bone and place on warm plates. Slice the breasts cross-wise and fan the slices on the plates. Drizzle with the sauce and serve immediately.

MISE EN PLACE

1 recipe for Chinese Lacquered Duck (recipe follows)

FOR THE DUCK

2 ducks, 5 pounds each

4 cups coarse (kosher) salt

2 cups honey

1/4 cup sugar

2 tablespoons unsalted butter

1/2 cup fresh orange juice

1/2 cup strong black coffee (optional)

1/4 cup coffee liqueur

1 teaspoon cornstarch

In some ways, this is a 'modern' version of a timeless recipe. The main difference is that I've shortened the time it takes to prepare it and reduced the portion sizes – but all the ingredients and decadent flavors are still here.

MAKE THE CASSOULET

Soak the cannellini beans overnight in 2 inches of water to cover. Rinse and strain the beans. In a heavy 2-quart pot, place the beans, slab bacon and onion. Cover with water and bring to a boil over high heat. Reduce the heat and simmer for 1 1/2 - 2 hours, or until the beans are tender. Occasionally skim the fat that rises to the top and discard. Remove the onion and slab bacon. Strain the beans and rinse under cold water.

In a sauté pan over high heat, render the bacon until it becomes soft and translucent, which is the stage just before it begins to crisp. Add the shallots and cook for 20 seconds, stirring or moving the pan constantly. Add the garlic and cook for 10 more seconds. Add the demi-glace and the beans, reduce over medium heat until the beans resemble a very thick porridge. Remove from the heat. Stir in the tomato and chives. Season with salt and pepper. Reserve on the stove over low heat, covered.

Finish the confit according to recipe directions.

ASSEMBLY

Spoon the cassoulet into the center of 4 plates. Place the crisped duck confit leg or thigh on top of the cassoulet. Garnish with a small amount of mesclun. Serve immediately.

MISE EN PLACE

Duck Confit (see page 71)

INGREDIENTS

8 ounces dried cannellini beans

1 ounce slab bacon

1/2 medium yellow onion, left intact at the root

2 ounces diced applewood bacon

1 shallot, diced

1 clove fresh garlic, diced

1 cup demi-glace

1 tablespoon peeled, seeded and diced tomato

1 teaspoon finely chopped chives

salt and pepper

DUCK CONFIT
on Mission Fig Prosciutto Flatbread with Feta Cheese

Duck confit is my favorite way to eat duck. Think of this dish as a type of pizza with Italian prosciutto and a bit of fig conserve for sweetness all topped by the crispy duck confit. For entertaining, lay out all the elements and let people build their own.

TO MAKE THE FLATBREAD DOUGH

Place the flour, salt, yeast and honey in a mixer with the dough hook attachment. While the mixer is turning on low, slowly add the water and oil. Knead at a slow speed until the dough is smooth, but firm. Divide the dough into 8 balls, about 2-1/2 ounces each. Cover with a damp towel and allow the dough to rise for 1 – 2 hours in a warm place or until double in volume. Scatter some flour on a clean work surface. Roll the dough out very thin. This dough doesn't have to be shaped in a perfect round. Actually, the more obtuse and random the shape, the more rustic and better it will look.

TO MAKE THE FIG CONSERVE

In a 2-quart saucepan, cook the onion, shallots and garlic over high heat until the onions are softened. Add the vinegar, port, sugar and chicken stock and bring to a simmer. When bubbling, add the figs. Cook until the mixture is thick and jam-like. Refrigerate in a sterile container, the conserve will keep for up to 2 weeks.

TO BAKE THE FLATBREAD

Preheat oven to 500°. Place the rolled out dough on a sheetpan sprinkled with corn-meal. Evenly and thinly distribute the fig preserves on the top of the dough. Bake for 4 minutes and remove from the oven. Place 1/2 of the feta cheese and 1/2 of the prosciutto randomly on the focaccia. Return to the oven and cook until browned, about 5-6 minutes. Remove from the oven and place on a serving plate. Place the rest of the feta and prosciutto over the focaccia and sprinkle with julienned scallions. Put the crisped duck confit on top and serve.

MISE EN PLACE

Duck Confit

Flatbread Dough (recipe follows)

3/4 cup Fig Conserve (recipe follows)

4 ounces thinly sliced Parma Prosciutto

1 sprig rosemary

2 scallions cut into a lengthwise julienne

2 tablespoons extra virgin olive oil

FOR THE FLATBREAD DOUGH

4 cups all-purpose flour

2 1/2 teaspoons fresh yeast

2 teaspoons salt

2 teaspoons honey

2 teaspoons extra virgin olive oil

1 3/4 cup lukewarm water

Additional flour for rolling

FOR THE FIG CONSERVE

1 yellow onion, diced

2 shallots, diced

1 teaspoon chopped garlic

1 cup balsamic vinegar

1/2 cup ruby red port

1/2 cup sugar

1/2 cup chicken stock

1 1/2 cups fresh mission figs or 1 1/4 cup dried mission figs

DUCK CONFIT

As I don't mind mentioning again, duck confit is my favorite way to eat duck. It cooks in its own juices while remaining crispy on the outside. Confit means sweet preservers (in this case, the duck preserved in its own fat). Properly chilled and stored, the duck confit will keep for up to a month.

Place all of the ingredients except duck-fat in a stainless steel pan or bowl, tossing thoroughly. Cover with plastic wrap and allow to marinate for 2 days. Re-toss the duck every 12 hours.

Preheat the oven to 275°. Barely heat a large, deep frying pan over low heat. Place the fat or oil in the pan and warm up slightly. While heating, remove the duck from the bowl, scraping off any herbs and spices with your hands. Place the duck in the warmed oil. The duck should be completely submerged in the oil. Bring to a slow simmer and place in the oven. Cook the duck for 2 1/2 - 3 hours, or until tender. (Insert a knife into the thigh and if there is no resistance, the duck is sufficiently cooked.) Remove from the oven and allow to cool. Cover the duck with plastic wrap and refrigerate until ready to use. If stored in this manner, the confit will keep for up to one month. The oil acts as a preservative. Confiture means "candied," which also means preserved in sugar. Although this duck is not sweet, it is preserved in it's own fat, hence the term "confit." The fat that is left behind is called "rendered duck fat" and is excellent for roasting potatoes and sautéing other items.

TO REHEAT AND SERVE THE DUCK CONFIT

Preheat oven to 425°. Carefully remove the 4 pieces of duck from the oil. Scrape as much of the congealed oil from the duck as possible. Take 3 tablespoons of the duck fat and heat it in an oven-proof non-stick pan over medium heat. When the oil is hot, place the duck in the pan, skin side up. Continue to heat for 2 minutes then turn the pieces over so they are skin side down. Place the pan in the oven and bake for 20 minutes, or until the skin becomes crispy. Remove the crisped duck from the pan and allow the fat to drain from the ducks on a paper towel.

INGREDIENTS

Legs and thighs from 1 Long Island duck

6 cloves of garlic, peeled and crushed

2 sprigs rosemary

1 bunch fresh thyme

1 tablespoon whole black peppercorns

2 tablespoons kosher salt

4 bay leaves

8 cups duck fat or vegetable oil

This is the way chicken has always been fried in my family. It comes out very crispy with the flavor of all the herbs. I mentioned this would be part of my last meal, and I mean it. Embellish with Southern favorites – fried okra, mashed potatoes, biscuits, etc.

Mix all ingredients for the marinade in a large bowl, and add to the cut up chicken. Cover with plastic film and let marinate for 3 days. Remove the chicken from marinade.

Preheat 350°. Preheat a large cast iron pot or heavy gauge pot and fill with 6 cups of vegetable frying oil. Dredge the chicken in the flour. Shake off the excess flour; carefully place the chicken in the oil. You will need to turn the chicken every few minutes to evenly cook. When the pieces of chicken float to the surface they should be done. Remove and drain on a wire rack or paper towel.

INGREDIENTS

4 pound chicken, cut into 10 pieces:

2 wing / breast parts

2 breast pieces

2 legs

2 thighs

2 backs

3 cups of flour

FOR THE MARINADE

1 quart water, room temperature

2 eggs

1 sprig fresh rosemary

1 sprig fresh thyme

2 bay leaves

2 tablespoons kosher salt

1 tablespoon black pepper

1 tablespoon garlic powder

1 teaspoon paprika

1 teaspoon cayenne pepper

1 tablespoon Worcestershire

1 teaspoon Louisiana hot sauce

GRAMMA'S CHICKEN *with Yukon Gold Potato Purée and Spaghetti Vegetables*

Serves 2

American version of classic French dish where chicken is first sautéed then braised (the sauce keeps the chicken moist). Great with roasted or puréed potatoes. For mashed or puréed potatoes, I only use Yukon gold; their buttery natural flavor is unsurpassed.

TO MAKE THE POTATOES

Submerge the potatoes into salted water and boil for 25 minutes or until the potatoes are tender. Strain the potatoes. Add the butter and rice the potatoes. Add 1/2 cup to 1 cup cream to the buttered potatoes. Season with salt and pepper; these should be very rich and luxurious. Keep warm in the pan, covered with a towel.

TO MAKE VEGETABLES

Sauté the carrots, squash and zucchini in butter in a large sauté pan until slightly wilted (about 2 minutes). Do not overcook. Season with salt and pepper to taste.

TO MAKE THE CHICKEN

Preheat oven to 425°. In a non-stick pan sauté the 4 pieces of chicken on each side until lightly brown. Add the bacon, onion and mushrooms and sauté for 1-2 minutes. Deglaze the pan with the white wine and reduce by two-thirds. Add demi-glace, brown chicken stock and herbs. Bring to a simmer, cover with aluminum foil and place the pan in the oven. Baste the chicken every 6-7 minutes until the done, about 30 minutes total. Remove the pan from the oven and let chicken rest for 10 minutes. Strain the sauce off into a fat separator and pour the rendered sauce into a clean saucepan. Reduce until it coats the back of a spoon.

ASSEMBLY

Place a large spoonful of potatoes in a bowl. Place the thigh / leg piece on top of the potatoes, place chicken breast over the thigh leg piece. Spoon the Grandma sauce over the chicken. Twirl the spaghetti vegetables around a fork and place on top of the chicken breast.

MISE EN PLACE

1 chicken, 4 pound, preferably free range, wings removed, boned and cut into four quarters

Yukon Gold Potato Purée (recipe follows)

Spaghetti Vegetables (recipe follows)

FOR THE CHICKEN

12 large mushrooms, quartered

2 ounces slab bacon, cut into 1/4" dice and cooked until crisp

12 pearl onions, peeled

1 cup brown chicken stock

1 cup demi-glace

1/2 cup white wine

1 sprig fresh thyme

1 bay leaf

salt and freshly ground black pepper

FOR THE YUKON GOLD POTATO PURÉE

1-1/2 pounds Yukon gold potatoes, peeled and quartered

1 cup of heavy cream

1 pound unsalted butter

FOR THE SPAGHETTI VEGETABLES

2 tablespoons butter

1 peeled jumbo carrot, cut into a spaghetti-length julienne

1 yellow squash, seeded and cut into a spaghetti-length julienne

1 zucchini, seeded and cut into a spaghetti-length julienne

GOAT CHEESE STUFFED CHICKEN BREAST

The key is to leave the skin of the chicken breast attached. Stuff the herbed goat cheese under the skin. (This not only adds flavor but produces a nice melted 'ooze' in contrast to the crispy chicken skin.) Roquefort or mozzarella would also work.

TO MAKE LENTILS

Place the lentils, carrots, celery, potato, shallots, bacon and garlic in a hot sauté pan. Add demi-glace and cook until almost all liquid has been reduced. Stir in the cheese and cook until the mixture is thick. Reserve in a warm place.

TO MAKE PESTO

Place the sun-dried tomatoes, basil, garlic, and parmesan cheese into a food processor or the grinder of a kitchen-aid type mixer. Grind the ingredients into a bowl. Then slowly add the extra virgin olive oil. Keep in a sterile container. The pesto can keep up to 2 weeks properly covered.

TO PREPARE CHICKEN

Lift the skin up from chicken by gently sliding a finger under it. Place equal amounts of goat cheese under the skin of the chicken. Gently pat the goat cheese down so there is not a mound of goat cheese in one spot. Season with salt and pepper to taste. Reserve, covered in the refrigerator.

TO MAKE SAVOY CABBAGE

Remove outer leaves from the Savoy cabbage. You will need 8-12 leaves. Cook the leaves in boiling water until just tender about 20-30 seconds. Immediately remove the cabbage from the water and place in an ice bath. Remove the stem from the outer cabbage leaves, trying to leave the cabbage leaf intact as much as possible. Pat the leaves dry.

TO MAKE PURSE

Using a 2 or 3-ounce ladle, line the inside of the ladle with the cabbage. The leaves extend out of the ladle. Fill the cabbage lined ladle with the cooked lentil / potato mixture. Pack the lentils tightly. Fold the outer leaves over the pressed lentils. Carefully remove purse from ladle, it should look like a dome when removed. Preheat an oven to 400°; place the lentil purse onto a non- stick pan. Drizzle with 4 tablespoons of demi-glace and cook until the purses are warm, about 15 minutes. Reserve.

MISE EN PLACE

4 single-lobe, chicken breasts, 6 ounces each, skin on

8 ounces goat cheese

6 ounces Sun-dried Tomato Pesto (recipe follows)

4 Lentil / Cabbage Purses (recipe follows)

FOR THE PESTO

6 ounces sun-dried tomatoes, rehydrated in warm water

1/2 cup of basil, leaves only

4 cloves peeled garlic

1/2 cup Parmigiano-Reggiano cheese

1 cup extra virgin olive oil

salt and freshly ground black pepper

FOR THE LENTIL CABBAGE PURSE

8 ounces cooked green lentils

2 ounces carrot brunoise

2 ounces celery brunoise

4 ounces peeled and fine diced potato, boiled until tender

2 ounces cooked finely diced applewood smoked bacon

1 teaspoon finely chopped garlic

1 cup demi-glace

2 teaspoons Parmigiano-Reggiano cheese

salt and freshly ground black pepper

8-10 outer leaves of a Savoy cabbage

TO MAKE CHICKEN

Heat a non-stick pan until it begins to smoke. Add 2 tablespoons of vegetable oil to the pan. Place the chicken breast skin side down in the pan and lightly brown. Turn the breast over and place in a preheated 400° oven. Bake for 15-20 minutes until the chicken breast are almost cooked. Remove the chicken breast from the oven and liberally add equal amounts of the sun-dried tomato pesto to the top of each breast. Return the chicken breast to the oven and cook for 5 more minutes.

ASSEMBLY

Place a lentil purse on a plate at the 12 o'clock position on the plate. Place the cooked chicken breast next to the purse and serve.

Spaetzle is the German equivalent of pasta, extruded into boiling water and then browned in a pan. It's seasoned with lots of cracked pepper. If fresh black-eyed peas are not available, use frozen (never canned). The 'heat' in this dish comes from chili oil (which can be purchased).

TO MAKE BLACK-EYED PEAS

Cook the black-eyed peas in water with the smoked ham hock until the black-eyed peas begin to become tender (35-40 minutes). Strain the peas under cold water. Remove the ham hock (it may be saved for later use). Mix all other ingredients with the black-eyed peas and reserve.

TO MAKE RED-EYE GRAVY

Smithfield ham is the best ham for red-eye gravy. It has a salty, rich flavor that imparts a smoky, lightly salty flavor to the gravy. Place the shaved Smithfield ham pieces in a hot pan. Move the ham pieces around after they have browned. Pour in the coffee and scrape the pan to loosen the drippings. Add the water and reduce by 1/2. Add the optional brown chicken stock and cool until the sauce coats the back of a spoon. Reserve.

TO GRILL THE QUAIL

Preheat grill. The quail will cook much more rapidly since it is mostly deboned. The quail should be cooked to medium-rare to medium (135°-140°) so it does not dry out. Season the quail and grill on each side for 4 minutes. Remove from the grill and allow the quail to rest.

ASSEMBLY

Mix the 3 ounces of the spaetzle with the black-eyed pea salad. Adjust the seasoning. Place the spaetzle, and the pea salad on the middle of a plate. Place the cooled quail on top of the salad. Drizzle red-eye gravy around the salad. Garnish with a fresh thyme and sage bouquet.

MISE EN PLACE

Black-eyed Pea Salad (recipe follows)

Chili Oil (recipe follows)

Red Eye Gravy (recipe follows)

Grilled quail

Spaetzle (see page144)

FOR THE BLACK-EYED PEA SALAD

4 ounces frozen or fresh black-eyed peas

1 smoked ham hock

1 teaspoon red bell pepper brunoise

1 teaspoon yellow bell pepper

1/2 teaspoon jalapeño pepper – brunoise

1/2 teaspoon brunoise red onion

1 teaspoon diced tomato concassé

2 teaspoon vegetable oil

1 teaspoon champagne vinegar

salt and pepper

1 teaspoon of chili oil

FOR THE CHILI OIL

4 tablespoons chili flakes

1 cup of vegetable oil

FOR THE RED-EYE GRAVY

8 ounces shaved Smithfield ham

1/2 cup water

1/4 cup coffee

1/4 cup brown chicken stock (optional)

ROASTED QUAIL
with Marinated Tomato, Eggplant and Tomatillo Sauce

This is a multi-cultural dish combining Mexico (tomatillo), the Southwest (quail) and the Mediterranean (tomato and eggplant). The presentation results in wonderful colors. You also learn how to make a very quick tomatillo sauce.

In a large non-reactive dish, mix 1/4 cup of the balsamic vinegar and the honey. Place the sage leaves on the breast meat of the quail and add the quail to the marinade. Coat the birds completely with the marinade. Let marinate for 1 hour.

In a medium skillet, heat 1-1/2 tablespoons of the olive oil over low heat. Add garlic and cook, stirring for one minute. Transfer the eggplant and garlic to a non-reactive bowl and let cool to room temperature. Fold in the tomatoes, lemon juice and remaining 1 tablespoon balsamic vinegar. Season with salt and white pepper to taste. Set aside.

In a medium saucepan of boiling water, blanch the tomatillo for 3 minutes to soften. Drain well and puree in a food processor. Set aside.

In a medium non-reactive saucepan, heat the remaining 2-1/2 teaspoons olive oil over moderate heat. Stir in the onion and cook until softened, about 4 minutes. Stir in the chicken stock, serrano chile and sugar. Stir in the tomatillo puree and bring it to boil. Season with coriander, salt and white pepper to taste.

Preheat the boiler. Season the marinated quail with salt and white pepper, place skin side up on a broiling pan. Broil, rotating the pan for about 3 minutes; the breast meat should remain pink. Spoon the tomato and eggplant mixture in the center of each warmed plate and place a quail on top. Spoon the tomatillo sauce around.

INGREDIENTS

1/4 cup plus 1 tablespoon balsamic vinegar

2 tablespoons honey

4 sage leaves, torn in pieces

4 partially boned quail, butterflied

2 tablespoons plus 1 teaspoon extra virgin olive oil

1 tablespoon minced garlic

1 cup diced eggplant (1/2" pieces)

3 fresh plum tomatoes – peeled, seeded and finely diced

1/2 teaspoon fresh lemon juice .

salt and freshly ground white pepper

10 tomatillos, cored

2 tablespoons minced onion

1 1/2 tablespoons chicken stock or canned broth

1 teaspoon minced serrano chile

pinch of sugar

1 tablespoon minced cilantro

SEAFOOD

THE ENDLESS POSSIBILITIES OF FISH

"The success of any fish recipe starts the moment you purchase the fish."

I'm no exception to the maxim – chefs love to cook fish. The basic quality of fish – its mild flavor – allows you to create virtually an infinite number of dishes. It's like having a blank canvas and the freedom to paint with any color, or in this case, flavor. Hopefully, with my recipes, you'll be turning out works of art.

The success of any fish recipe starts when you purchase the fish. Being in Dallas, I don't have easy access to a conventional fish market, but we have an incredible fishmonger who flies in pristinely fresh fish daily. I'm convinced that even if you live in a land locked city as we do, the miracle of modern aviation has made the procurement of quality seafood an easy task.

Still, you have to trust your eye and especially your nose. Some of the things I look for are glossy scales, clear eyes, vibrant red meat (for tuna), and most important of all, an absence of fish smell. Even the slightest smell is unacceptable. I supply my restaurants with an array of seafood from Atlantic turbot to sushi grade big eye tuna to black cod from Alaska. Scallops are perhaps my very favorite seafood item with which to work. Unfortunately, fresh diver scallops are one of the few things you may have problems obtaining. When available, we have these jumbo sea scallops flown in from New England. (Store-bought scallops in preservative solution, pale in comparison.) When it comes to oysters, I've discovered that West Coast Kumomotas are unsurpassed. They have a refreshing, fruit-like flavor in addition to a clean briny taste. As a note: avoid cocktail sauces when serving or eating oysters. Instead use a simple mignonette with shallots and cracked black pepper. (See Appetizers for recipe).

CRABMEAT ENCHILADA
with Pasilla-Ancho Chile Sauce and Jicama Salad

It's not unusual for patrons to order two orders of this appetizer to serve as an entree. In fact, it's been my number one selling appetizer since The Mercury opened. If you like, you can substitute shrimp for crab.

FOR THE TORTILLAS AND BASTING SAUCE

In a saucepan, bring the chile powder, cumin, paprika, cayenne, garlic salt, kosher salt, vegetable oil and water to a boil. Reduce the heat to low and keep warm. Heat the cup of vegetable oil to 350° in a sauté pan. Slide a tortilla into the hot oil. Lightly shake the tortilla back and forth until it becomes pliable. Remove the tortilla from the pan and dip in the paprika mixture to coat, shaking off the excess. Place on a plate loosely covered with a sheet of plastic wrap. Repeat with the other tortillas. Reserve.

FOR THE CHILE SAUCE

Heat the butter in a quart saucepan. When the butter begins to brown, add the ancho and pasilla chile pieces, onion, carrot and celery. Sauté until the vegetables become limp. Add the tomato paste, cumin, paprika and flour. Stir well and add the vegetable stock. Reduce the heat and simmer for 20. Add the cilantro and continue to cook for another 3 minutes. Place the hot sauce in a blender and purée until smooth, about 3 minutes. (Due to the physics of heat, if you cover the blender with the plastic cover and blend, the hot air will expand and force the top right off the blender. To avoid this, turn the blender on and slowly add the sauce.) Strain the sauce; add the lime juice and season with salt and pepper. Reserve and keep warm.

FOR THE JICAMA SALAD

Place all of the julienned vegetables in a bowl. Add the cilantro, chives, olive oil and lime juice. Toss well and season with salt and pepper. Reserve and chill.

FINAL PREPARATION AND ASSEMBLY

Clean the crabmeat of any shell fragments. Heat the butter in a sauté pan. When the butter begins to brown, add the crabmeat and sauté for 30 seconds. Add the spinach leaves and continue to cook until the spinach wilts. Add 1/2 the jack cheese and mix well. Reserve and keep warm.

Preheat oven to 400°. Place the corn tortillas on a flat surface and place equal amounts of the crabmeat/spinach mixture in the center of each. Carefully roll up the tortilla like a large cigar. It should be snug, but not too tight. Place each tortilla on a

MISE EN PLACE

4 thick corn tortillas

1/2 cup Tortilla Basting Sauce (recipe follows)

3/4 cup Jicama Salad (recipe follows)

1 cup Pasilla-Ancho Chile Sauce (recipe follows)

1 cup vegetable oil

1/4 cup crème fraiche

1 cup jumbo lump crabmeat

1 tablespoon butter

3/4 cup Monterrey jack cheese, grated

1 cup spinach, well cleaned

FOR THE TORTILLA BASTING SAUCE

1/2 teaspoon chile powder

1/2 teaspoon cumin

1/2 teaspoon paprika

Pinch cayenne pepper

1/4 teaspoon garlic salt

1/4 teaspoon kosher salt

1 tablespoon vegetable oil

2 cups water

FOR THE PASILLA-ANCHO CHILE SAUCE (MAKES 1 PINT)

4 tablespoons butter

2 dried ancho chiles, seeded and chopped

1 dried pasilla chile, seeded and chopped

1/2 medium yellow onion, roughly chopped

1/2 large carrot, peeled and roughly chopped

1 rib celery, roughly chopped

3 cloves garlic

1/4 cup tomato paste

1 teaspoon cumin

1 tablespoon paprika

3 ounces flour

2 cups vegetable stock

2 ounces fresh cilantro

juice of 2 limes

warm serving plate. Sprinkle the remaining jack cheese on top of the enchiladas. Place the plates in the oven for 1 – 2 minutes until the cheese begins to melt. (This may also be done under the broiler.) Remove plates (wear your mitts!) from the oven and ladle 2 ounces of the chile sauce over each enchilada. Drizzle each of the plates with the crème fraiche. Place equal amounts of the jicama salad on top of the enchiladas and serve immediately.

FOR THE JICAMA SALAD

1 small Jicama, peeled, sliced and cut into a 3" long julienne

1/2 large carrot, peeled and cut into a fine 3" long julienne

1 zucchini, cut into a fine julienne 3" long, with green skin attached.

1/2 red bell pepper – cut into a fine julienne, 3" long

1 tablespoon cilantro leaves

1 teaspoon minced chives

1 tablespoon extra virgin olive oil

juice of 2 limes

salt & pepper

HALIBUT WRAPPED IN BACON

Serves 4

The title of this recipe says it all. Halibut is a unique white flesh fish with a natural, rich, buttery flavor. The bacon adds another dimension of taste and importantly keeps the fish moist. Italian pancetta may be substituted for the bacon.

INGREDIENTS

2 russet potatoes

3/4 cup cream

4 Italian plum tomatoes

2 cloves garlic

6 tablespoons butter

4 ounces extra virgin olive oil

20 slices bacon

4 halibut filets

15 leaves of basil

salt and pepper

TO MAKE
Preheat oven to 450°. Peel the potatoes and cut into slices. Cover in cold salted water and bring to a boil. Simmer for 25 minutes or until tender. Remove from water and puree with a little added cooking water, cream and 2 tablespoons of butter. Season with salt and pepper to taste.

Cut ends of tomatoes and place on an oiled roasting pan. Cut garlic into thin slices and insert into tomato cavity. Sprinkle with salt and pepper and drizzle with olive oil. Roast in the oven for 20 minutes and cut each in half. Set aside in a pan with 2 tablespoons of butter and keep warm.

Preheat oven to 500°. Wrap halibut with bacon, sauté in a non-stick pan, then place in oven for 9 minutes.

ASSEMBLY
Julienne the basil and add it to the tomatoes. Spread the potato puree on a platter. Place halibut on top and sauce with the tomatoes. Serve immediately.

This fish has been my biggest seller at Citizen since day one. It flakes into sections, which makes it very easy to eat with chopsticks (the beautiful caramelized color is due to the sugar and miso marinade). Black cod is caught in the cold waters of Alaska (it's also known as Sable fish or Sand fish.) If it's unavailable, substitute Chilean Sea Bass or Halibut.

MISE EN PLACE

4 portions of black cod, 6 ounces each, bones removed

1 pint of Miso Marinade (recipe follows)

1 cup Miso glaze (recipe follows)

4 pickled whole ginger root

4 bamboo leaves optional

FOR THE MARINADE

Mix all ingredients for marinade. Allow the fish to marinate for at least 12 hours.

FOR THE MARINADE

1/2 cup of blonde Miso

1/4 cup mirin

1/2 cup sugar

1/2 cup water

1/4 cup sake

FOR THE GLAZE

Sweat the shallot for 1-2 minutes. Add the mirin, sugar, sake and miso. Bring to a boil and strain. Reserve at room temperature.

FOR THE GLAZE

1 shallot sliced

5 ounces miso

1/4 cup mirin

1/8 cup sake

1/2 cup sugar

1 ounce vegetable oil

TO COOK THE FISH

Remove the marinated black cod from marinade, place fish on a sheetpan or in a non-stick pan. Turn on the broiler and broil fish for 7-8 minutes. The fish should take on a lovely caramelized, lacquered appearance. This is caused by the sugar in the marinade. Remove from broiler and allow fish to rest for 1-2 minutes.

ASSEMBLY

Place a bamboo leaf on each plate; place the fish on top of the bamboo leaf. Garnish with the pickled ginger root. Dot the plate with the miso sauce and serve.

I'll say it again, diver scallops are the finest seafood product available. But what I want you to focus on in this recipe is the consommé. To prepare it, you need to have already made the lobster stock (see Basics). This recipe takes time, but the finished product is well worth it.

TO MAKE THE CONSOMMÉ

Coarsely chop the celery, onion and carrot in a food processor fitted with a steel blade. Remove from the processor and mix the egg whites into the vegetables; the egg whites will help to clarify the lobster stock. Place this mixture and lobster stock in a 1-gallon stock pot and stir well. Bring the stock to a simmer. The egg white/vegetable mixture will float to the top. Simmer for 1-2 hours and add the brandy. When the stock (or now, the consommé) has cooked down to 2 cups, gently pass the stock through cheesecloth lined strainer into a sterile container. When straining, do not push down on the vegetables or the consommé will be cloudy; just let it strain on its own. Season with salt and pepper to taste. Reserve and keep warm.

TO PREPARE THE OYSTERS

Have your fishmonger shuck your oysters with their natural juices and keep cold until final preparation. Gently poach the oysters in their liquid for 20 seconds until just cooked. They are ready when the ridges of the oysters begin to curl.

TO PREPARE THE MUSSELS

Clean the mussels of their beard and any outside dirt. Place 1 cup white wine and finely chopped shallots in a sauté pan. Add the mussels to the pan, place over high heat. Cover the pan with a lid and cook mussels until their shells begin to open. Strain the liquid from the mussels. Save the mussel jus for another use. Remove the cooked mussels from their shells and reserve.

TO PREPARE THE SCALLOPS

Season the scallops with salt and pepper. Dry sauté the scallops over high heat for 2 minutes per side in a non-stick skillet. Remove the scallops from the pan and keep warm.

TO ASSEMBLE

Reheat the cooked vegetables with the lobster consommé in a saucepan. When the vegetables are warm, add the cooked mussels, lobster and oysters and reheat over very low heat. Place 3 scallops in the center of each of 4 shallow soup bowls. Place 1 piece of sea urchin roe on top of scallops. Divide the warm seafood and vegetables between the four plates. Gently pour the lobster consommé over the raw sea urchin. Top the sea urchin with caviar and sprinkle the shiso leaves around the consommé.

MISE EN PLACE

12 U-10 or larger dry scallops

12 Malpec or Bluepoint oysters

4 ounces sea urchin roe

2 dozen mussels

1 Maine lobster lobster, 1 pound

Lobster Consommé (recipe follows)

VEGETABLES

8 baby carrots, peeled and blanched

4 asparagus, peeled and blanched

1/4 cup edamame beans (soybeans)

2 Shiitake mushrooms, sliced

2 ounces bamboo shoots

6 ears baby corn

3 ounces Osetra caviar (optional)

5 shiso leaves, cut into a julienne (available at Japanese markets, optional)

FOR THE CONSOMMÉ

1 rib celery

1/2 Spanish onion

1 small carrot, peeled

2 quarts Lobster Stock (see Basics)

4 egg whites

3 ounces brandy

FLAMING GRILLED SCALLOP
with Asparagus Osetra Caviar and Warm Ponzu Sauce

Don't overlook the word 'flaming' in this recipe. A simple dish with a stunning presentation (every cook needs one flaming dish in their repertoire). You can either grill or sauté the scallops. The caviar and ponzu sauce both bump up the taste. A guaranteed crowd pleaser from the moment you walk into the room carrying a plate 'con fuego.'

FOR THE ASPARAGUS

Bring a pot of salted water to a boil and blanch the asparagus for 2-3 minutes or just until firm. Remove the asparagus from the water and place them in an ice water bath to stop the cooking process. When asparagus spears are sufficiently cool, remove from the ice water and pat lightly dry. Make 2 lengthwise cuts up the asparagus stem, stopping about 1/2 –inch short of the blossom end. Keep warm.

TO MAKE THE SCALLOPS

Combine the soy sauce, vinegar and the orange juice in a bowl; reserve.

TO MAKE THE SCALLOPS

Preheat a grill to high. If you are lucky enough to get jumbo scallops, you will see a muscle running along the side of the scallop. Just take your finger and gently separate these two, removing the muscle entirely. Season the scallop with salt, pepper and brush with extra virgin olive oil. Grill the scallops on each side for 1-2 minutes or until just opaque. Do not overcook. Remove from the grill and reserve, keeping warm.

TO ASSEMBLE

Place a 4-ounce mound of rock salt on each of the serving plates. Place a cleaned scallop shell on top of the rock salt. Pour 2 tablespoons of ponzu sauce in the scallop shell. Put 1 scallop in the center of the shell on the sauce. Fan the asparagus stem and arc it around the scallop. Place one ounce of caviar atop each scallop.

Now for the extreme food part: You will need to do the following rather quickly. Pour equal amounts of the alcohol around the rock salt on each plate. Using a fireplace match, stand back and light. Serve while flaming.
WARNING: Do not use a short match or lighter to light the rum. There are other factors at work here, like the temperature of the kitchen and the rum, so when you light the plate, it could flame up pretty high. If you do as instructed, you will have a nice controlled burn and nobody gets hurt. I recommend practicing.

MISE EN PLACE

4 jumbo diver scallops

1 cup Ponzu Sauce (recipe follows)

8 jumbo asparagus, peeled and trimmed

4 ounces Osetra caviar

4 scallop shells, sterilized

2 tablespoons chopped julienne of scallion

1 pound rock salt

3 ounces 151 Rum (or other liquor with a high alcohol content)

salt & pepper

FOR THE PONZU SAUCE

1/2 cup lite soy sauce

1/2 cup rice wine vinegar

Juice of 1 Valencia orange

CRAB AND SHRIMP POTATO NAPOLEON
with Spicy Avocado Sauce and Crème Fraiche

Perfect for summer, this cold dish is easier to prepare than it appears (it's a favorite lunch item at The Mercury). Once the avocado sauce and the mayonnaise are made, the shrimp are cooked, and the potato wafers are fried, the dish is easy and fun to assemble.

TO MAKE THE AVOCADO SAUCE

Heat the 2 tablespoons vegetable oil in a 2 quart saucepan. When the oil begins to smoke, add the onion, shallot and garlic. Lightly sauté over medium heat. Add the avocados and peppers, sautéing for 5 minutes more. Add the vegetable stock, reduce the heat and simmer for 15 – 20 minutes. Add the cilantro, cream and simmer for 5 more minutes. Add the sauce to a running blender and purée until smooth, about 3 minutes. Press through a fine sieve with the back of a spoon or spatula. Stir in the lime juice and taste to season with salt and pepper.

MISE EN PLACE

1/2 pound jumbo lump crabmeat

16 boiled Colossal Shrimp (recipe follows)

3/4 cup Tomato Mayonnaise (recipe follows)

1 1/4 cup Avocado Sauce (recipe follows)

12 Potato Wafers (recipe follows)

3 ounces crème fraiche

1/2 cup diced tomato concassé

4 tablespoons minced chives

FOR THE AVOCADO SAUCE

2 tablespoons vegetable oil

1/2 yellow onion, roughly cut

TO MAKE THE MAYONNAISE

Place the egg yolks, mustard and vinegar in a food processor. With the motor running, slowly add the vegetable oil until the mayonnaise is thick. Scrape the mayonnaise into a bowl and add the ketchup, brandy, Worcestershire and tomatoes. The sauce should be a pinkish-orange color. Taste and season with salt and pepper. Cover with plastic wrap and chill.

TO COOK THE SHRIMP

Place the onion, celery, herbs, salt, wine, peppercorns and 2 quarts of water in a 4-quart pot. Squeeze the lemon halves into the water and throw those in too. Bring to a boil and simmer for 20 minutes. Drop the shrimp into the simmering water and cook for 4 – 5 minutes or until the shrimp are opaque. Do not overcook. There's nothing worse than overly stiff, dry shrimp and these puppies are too good (and expensive) to ruin. Remove the shrimp with a slotted skimming spoon and drop into a bowl of ice water to stop the cooking. When cool, peel and devein the shrimp. Discard the tail as well. Reserve in a cool place.

TO MAKE THE POTATO WAFERS

Slice the potatoes lengthwise on a mandoline into thin flat slices about 1/8" thin. Run the potato slices under cool water to remove as much of the potato's natural starch as possible. Pat dry. Heat the vegetable oil (in a saucepan large enough to accommodate the length of a potato slice) to 340°. Fry the potato slices in small batches until they are crispy and golden, about 3 minutes. Drain on paper towels; reserve. Place in an airtight tin if they are to sit out longer than a few hours.

TO ASSEMBLE

Remove any crab shells from the jumbo lump crabmeat. Dice the cooked shrimp into 1/2" cubes. Place the crabmeat and shrimp in a bowl and mix with 8 tablespoons of the tomato mayonnaise. Season with salt and pepper.

Ladle 3 ounces each of the avocado sauce onto the center of 4 plates. Place one potato wafer on top of the sauce. Spread a spoonful of the shrimp/crab mixture on top of the wafer. Repeat this process 2 more times, ending with the 3rd wafer. This should resemble a layered napoleon. Drizzle the plate with crème fraiche and sprinkle with chopped chives around the plate. Serve at once.

1 shallot, peeled and diced

1 garlic clove

3 ripe Haas avocados, cut in half, seeded, skinned and roughly cut

3 serrano peppers, seeded and diced

2 cups vegetable stock

2 tablespoons fresh cilantro

Juice of 1 lime

1/2 cup heavy cream

salt & pepper

FOR THE TOMATO MAYONNAISE

3 egg yolks

1 tablespoon Dijon mustard

1/4 cup red wine vinegar

2 cups vegetable oil

1 tablespoon brandy

3 tablespoons ketchup

2 tablespoons tomato concassé

1 teaspoon Worcestershire sauce

salt & pepper

FOR THE SHRIMP

16 colossal shrimp (10 to 15 per pound)

1 small yellow onion, quartered

1 rib celery

1 teaspoon black peppercorns

1 bay leaf

1 sprig fresh thyme

2 teaspoons salt

1/2 cup white wine (optional)

2 quarts water

1 lemon, cut in half

FOR THE POTATO WAFERS

2 jumbo Idaho potatoes, peeled

2 cups vegetable oil

FRIED CALAMARI
with Spicy Tomato Risotto and Green Olive Tapenade

I have tried, but can not take this off my menu. (It has become too popular.) The risotto underneath the crisped calamari and the tangy tapenade purée make this classic a house favorite.

TO MAKE THE TAPENADE

Place the olives in a pan with 1 cup water. Bring to a boil and immediately strain the hot olives. Place the olives, garlic cloves, anchovy, basil, parsley and capers in a blender and purée. With the blender running, slowly trickle in the olive oil. Season with salt and pepper to taste. Remove from the blender and refrigerate. This can be stored in the refrigerator for up to 1 week.

TO MAKE THE MARINARA

Heat the oil in a non-reactive pan over medium-high heat. When the oil begins to smoke, add the onion and garlic. Lightly sweat the vegetables without browning. As soon as soon as the onions are translucent and soft, add the tomatoes and simmer for 20 minutes. Remove from the heat and add the herbs and the chili flakes. Pass the tomatoes through a ricer. Season with salt and pepper to taste. Reserve in a warm place.

TO MAKE THE RISOTTO

On a separate burner, heat the vegetable stock, keep over low heat and keep a ladle handy. Heat the butter in a non-reactive 3-quart saucepan over high heat. When the butter browns, add the onion and garlic. Stir until they begin to color. Add the rice and continue to stir until the rice begins to color. Deglaze the pan with the white wine. Add the herbs and reduce the heat to medium. When the wine has been absorbed, add the vegetable stock a little at a time, stirring constantly. The constant stirring and slow addition of liquid will allow the starch to emerge from the rice. When the risotto is 1/2 cooked, add 1/2 cup more stock and remove from the heat. Spread it on a shallow baking sheet. This will rapidly cool the risotto and prevent overcooking. Risotto can be made 2 days in advance.

TO MAKE THE CALAMARI

Remove the calamari from the milk (soaking them in milk tenderizes the calamari) and lightly toss with the cornstarch. Fry at 350° until lightly golden and crisp. Season with salt and pepper to taste. Reserve and keep warm. Place 1/2 cup of the marinara in a pan and add the risotto. Cook over medium heat and stir the risotto constantly.

MISE EN PLACE

Spicy Tomato Risotto (recipe follows)

6 ounces Spicy Marinara (recipe follows)

8 ounces Green Olive Tapenade (recipe follows)

1 recipe Fried Calamari (recipe follows)

FOR THE GREEN OLIVE TAPENADE

6 ounces pitted green manzanilla olives

4 cloves garlic, peeled

1 anchovy, rinsed

1 bunch fresh basil, leaves only

1 bunch Italian leaf parsley, leaves only

1 tablespoon capers, rinsed

3 ounces extra virgin olive oil

FOR THE SPICY MARINARA

2 tablespoons extra virgin olive oil

1 yellow onion, roughly cut

2 garlic cloves

20 peeled roma tomatoes, or 10 ounces whole canned peeled tomatoes

2 sprigs thyme

1 bunch fresh basil

1 bunch Italian flat leaf parsley

1 tablespoon red chili flakes

FOR THE RISOTTO

3 cups Vegetable Stock (see Basics)

2 tablespoons butter

1/2 medium yellow onion, diced

2 garlic cloves, minced

1 cup arborio rice

1/2 cup white wine

Add 1/2 cup warm vegetable stock. Continue stirring and add the parmigiano cheese and the butter. The risotto should be very rich and creamy in appearance.

ASSEMBLY

Divide the risotto equally in 4 shallow bowls, spooning the remaining spicy marinara around it. Place the calamari on top of the risotto. Drizzle the calamari with the green olive tapenade and serve immediately.

1 bay leaf

1 sprig thyme

salt & pepper

1/4 cup Parmigiano-Reggiano cheese

FOR THE CALAMARI

1 pound cleaned calamari, with tentacles, soaked in 1 cup milk for 2 days

3 tablespoons cornstarch

GRILLED SCALLOP
with Kumquat Fennel Glaze and Black Truffle Oil

My chef de cuisine at The Mercury Grill, Tim Bivens, helped create this dish. It's a surprising combination of sweet and sour tastes. Again, I sing the praises of the scallop which can be grilled like a piece of prime beef. The truffle oil adds a luxurious richness.

FOR THE GLAZE
Extract as much of the juice from the kumquats as possible. Place the kumquat juice, orange juice, lemon juice, freshly shaved fennel, sugar, vinegar and water in a 2-quart heavy gauge saucepan. Bring to a simmer and cook until the mixture resembles a thick glaze. Remove from the stove and add the sliced kumquats. Keep warm.

FOR THE SCALLOPS
Season the scallops with salt and pepper. Brush with vegetable oil and grill on each side for 2 minutes or until opaque. Reserve in a warm place to rest.

ASSEMBLY
Spoon 2 ounces of the kumquat glaze into the center of a shallow bowl. Place 3 of the scallops in the center. Sprinkle with shaved truffles and drizzle with black truffle oil. Garnish with the wild arugula and serve.

MISE EN PLACE

1 recipe Kumquat Glaze (recipe follows)

12 jumbo scallops

1 teaspoon truffle peelings

black truffle oil

3 ounces wild arugula (Selvetta if available)

salt & pepper

FOR THE KUMQUAT FENNEL GLAZE

8 ounces kumquats (2 kumquats reserved and sliced)

2 ounces fresh orange juice

4 ounces freshly shaved fennel

Juice of 1 lemon

4 ounces granulated sugar

1/4 cup rice wine vinegar

3 ounces granulated sugar

1 cup water

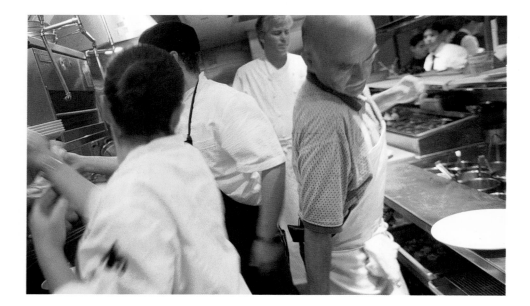

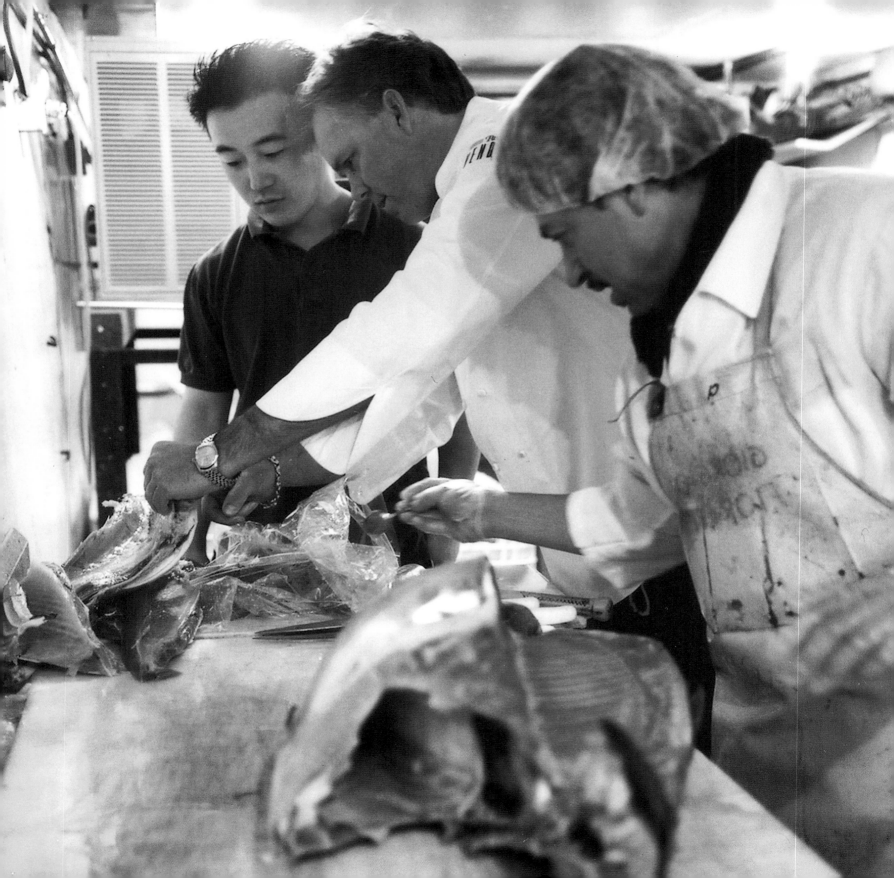

GRILLED YELLOW FIN TUNA
with Green Onion Noodle Cake

This Asian-influenced dish is centered around the green onion noodle cake. Think of this 'cake' as fresh pasta formed into a small cake – crispy on the outside and moist on the inside.

TO COOK THE TUNA

Preheat grill or broiler. Grill or broil the tuna steaks for 20 seconds on each side for rare tuna.

TO MAKE THE GREEN-ONION NOODLE CAKE

Preheat oven to 350°. Cook the angel-hair pasta in a large pot of boiling salted water about 2 minutes. Drain but do not rinse. Combine with chopped scallions. Use one tablespoon of butter to grease the bottom of an 8" inch cake pan. Transfer the pasta to the cake pan flattening it with spatula so that it is no more than 1/2" deep. Cut remaining butter into small pieces and strew across the top of the pasta. Place in the preheated oven for 5-10 minutes or just until the top is lightly browned. Turn the noodle cake over and repeat the process on the other side. Remove from the oven and let rest while you prepare the vinaigrette and tuna.

TO MAKE THE VINAIGRETTE

Peel and seed the tomatoes. Blend the peeled tomatoes with the extra virgin olive oil and vinegar. Add the minced serrano chili pepper. Mix well and season to taste.

TO MAKE TEMPURA GARNISH

It is best if the batter and scallops are chilled before frying. Prepare the tempura batter. Dip the scallops into the batter and deep fry in an inch of hot oil about 2 minutes, until crisp and golden. Drain on paper towels.

ASSEMBLY

In the center of the dinner plates, make a circle about 3" in diameter of overlapping thin cucumber slices. Cut the noodle cake into four wedges and place a wedge on top of each cucumber circle. Place the tuna steaks on top of the noodle cake wedges. Spoon the tomato vinaigrette around the edge of the plate and garnish the fish with bay scallop tempura. Serve immediately.

FOR THE TUNA

4 tablespoons olive oil

2 tablespoons finely chopped fresh green herbs

4 yellow fin tuna steaks, 5 ounces each

FOR THE GREEN NOODLE CAKE

3/4 pound fresh angel-hair pasta

4 whole scallions, very finely chopped

FOR THE VINAIGRETTE

1 cup extra virgin olive oil

1/3 cup tarragon vinegar

2 large ripe tomatoes

3 serrano chile peppers, seeded and finely minced

FOR THE GARNISH

12 bay scallops

1 cup tempura batter (see TK)

salt and pepper to taste

2 European cucumbers, thinly sliced

KATAIFI CRUSTED SHRIMP
with Green Olive Tapenade and Citron Pepper

Serves 4

Easy to prepare with a great crust – shredded phyllo dough. A nice light crunch. The tangy green olive tapenade is what is known in my business as an 'enhancer.' Very colorful presentation.

TO MAKE THE KATAIFI SHRIMP
Remove the kataifi from the package and carefully unwind onto the counter. Cover with a slightly damp towel so it will not dry out. Season the shrimp with salt and pepper. While holding the tail of the shrimp, carefully wrap the shrimp. The only exposed part should be the tail. Place on a sheet pan.

TO MAKE BALSAMIC GLAZE
Reduce 1/2 cup balsamic vinegar over low heat by two thirds. This will remove the vinegar flavor and turn the balsamic into a sweet/tart glaze.

Preheat the canola oil to 350°. Using a slotted spoon, slowly drop the shrimp in the oil in batches of 4 and fry until golden brown. About 2 – 3 minutes. Drain on paper towels. Reserve and keep warm.

ASSEMBLY
Place 1/4 cup of the tapenade on the center of each plate. Toss the bell peppers and citrus segments together. Place equal amounts of the fruit/pepper mixture on top of the tapenade. Place 3 of the shrimp around the center of the plate with the tails pointing outward. Drizzle with the balsamic glaze.

INGREDIENTS

12 U-15 shrimp, peeled and deveined

1 box Kataifi (shredded phyllo dough), thawed

2 quarts canola oil

8 ounces Green Olive Tapenade (see page 90)

2 roasted red bell peppers

2 roasted yellow bell peppers

2 Valencia oranges, sectioned

2 ruby red grapefruit, sectioned

2 tablespoons Balsamic Glaze

salt & pepper

LOBSTER *with Fava Bean Puree and Black Trumpet Mushrooms*

Serves 4

Since this is served in shallow soup bowls, you'll want to think of the fava bean puree as the 'soup.' In this case, a very bright green soup with a wonderful pea taste. Don't worry if you can't find the Black Trumpet mushroom (it's somewhat exotic). Remember: do not overcook the lobster.

In 4 gallon non-reactive stockpot, combine 1 gallon of cool water and the vinegar. Bring to a boil over high heat. Plunge the lobsters in the water, head first. Cover the pot and return to a boil. Boil the lobsters for 4 minutes. Remove them and set aside to cool. Discard the cooking water. Do not overcook the lobster or they will be tough and rubbery.

INGREDIENTS

2 tablespoons red wine vinegar

4 live lobsters, 1 pound each

1 tablespoon olive oil

1 pound chicken backs and or wings cut in pieces

1 sprig of fresh rosemary

3 garlic cloves, crushed

1 large shallot sliced

1/4 cup dry vermouth

Preheat the oven to 425°. Detach the lobster tails from the bodies. Twist off the claws and crack them. Remove the meat and set aside in a bowl. Using shears, cut along the underside of the tail shells. Separate the shells to release the meat and add to the bowl. Split the lobster bodies lengthwise and pull out and discard the cottony membranes. Set aside all the shells.

In a shallow non-reactive roasting pan, heat olive oil. Toss in the chicken parts and roast in the oven for 30 seconds. Add the reserved lobster shells, 1 rosemary sprig, garlic and shallots, roasting for 20 minutes. Stir occasionally. Add the vermouth and tomatoes. Roast for 10 minutes longer. Stir in the hot chicken stock and simmer in the oven for 30 minutes. Strain the liquid into small non-reactive saucepan; discard the solids. Cook the liquid over moderately high heat until reduced to 1/2 cup, about 10 minutes. Set the lobster glaze aside.

FOR THE FAVA BEAN PUREE

In a large saucepan, bring 4 cups of water to a boil over high heat. Add the fava beans and blanch for 30 seconds. Drain the beans in a colander and refresh under cold running water to stop the cooking. Using your fingers, peel the beans and discard the tough skins. In the same pan, melt 1-1/2 teaspoons of the butter over moderate heat. Add the onion and the remaining rosemary sprigs and cook, stirring occasionally until softened (about 5 minutes). Add the fava beans and 1/2 cup water and cook until the beans are tender (8-10 minutes). Discard the rosemary sprig. Scrape the fava beans into food processor. Add 2 tablespoons of the butter and puree until smooth. Season to taste with salt and pepper.

TO MAKE THE MUSHROOMS

In a medium skillet, melt 1 1/2 teaspoons of the butter over high heat. Add the mushrooms and sauté 1 to 2 minutes; season to taste. Remove from heat and keep warm.

ASSEMBLY

Re-warm the lobster glaze over moderate heat in a medium skillet. Stir the remaining 1 tablespoon butter and season with pepper to taste. Reduce the heat to very low, add the lobster meat and toss gently with a wooden spoon to warm through, about 2-3 minutes. Reheat the Fava bean puree in a double boiler over simmering water. Spoon the fava purée into the center of 4 large warmed shallow soup plates. Arrange the lobster over the puree and strain about 1-1/2 tablespoons of the glaze over each serving. Garnish with the mushrooms and serve at once.

2 plum tomatoes cut in cubes

3 cups chicken stock or canned low -sodium broth, heated

3 pound fresh fava beans, shelled

4 tablespoons unsalted butter

1 small onion coarsely chopped

salt and freshly ground black pepper

1/4 pound fresh black trumpet mushrooms trimmed, rinsed and patted dry

PEPPER CRUSTED TUNA *with Garlic Spinach, Cranberry Corn Galette and Chanterelle Mushroom Braise*

Without a doubt, this is my best selling entree at both Mercury restaurants. Think of it as a pepper crusted filet, but prepared with the finest quality tuna instead. For maximum results, cook the tuna to a 'cool' rare. It sits atop a cranberry-corn galette. The crisped spinach adds another dimension to the dish.

TO MAKE POTATOES

Cover the potatoes with cold water and place over a moderate heat and simmer until the potatoes are just cooked about 30 minutes. Strain the cooked potatoes and put them through a ricer. Place the riced potatoes in a large bowl and add the cranberries and chives. In a medium skillet heat half of the butter. When the butter begins to brown add the corn kernels and cook slowly for 2 minutes. Season with salt and pepper. Add the corn to the potato mixture and mix well; season to taste. Divide the potato mixture into 4 equal parts and form them into discs resembling hockey pucks. Reserve; galettes can be made one day in advance.

TO MAKE THE CHANTERELLE MUSHROOM BRAISE

Place butter in medium sauté pan, when butter begins to brown add the chanterelles and sauté for 1-2 minutes. Add the shallots and cook for an additional 30 seconds, add the vermouth and cook or reduce until almost all the liquid has evaporated. Add the demi-glace and cook until the sauce coats the back of a spoon. Season with salt and pepper and reserve in a warm place.

FOR THE TUNA

Season each side of the tuna with salt and lightly cover each side with cracked black pepper. Heat a large sauté pan up over medium heat; add 2 tablespoons vegetable oil to the pan. When the oil begins to smoke add the tuna to the pan, pepper side down first. Cook for about 1 minute and turn the tuna over and cook for 1 minute on the other side. Remove tuna from the pan and keep warm.

TO COOK THE GALETTE AND ASSEMBLE

Place a medium non-stick pan over moderate heat. Place the galettes in the pan disc side down and cook on each side for 2-3 minutes or until each side is golden brown. Remove the cooked galettes from the pan and place in the center of each plate. Place the seared rare tuna on top of the corn galette. Place the rest of the butter in a pan and sauté the spinach over a very high heat for 5-10 seconds. Add 1/4 teaspoon chopped garlic to the spinach. Season with salt and pepper. Place the spinach on top of the seared tuna, spoon the chanterelle mushroom braise around the tuna and serve.

INGREDIENTS

4-5 oz sushi quality tuna steaks, cut to resemble filets

2 tablespoons cracked black pepper

4 potato-corn galette

8 ounces chanterelle mushroom braise

1 cup Spinach

1/4 teaspoon chopped garlic

FOR THE POTATO CORN GALETTE

2 Large idaho potatoes peeled and cut into eights

1 Ear of corn, kernels removed

1/4 cup dried cranberries

2 tablespoon finely chopped chives

2 egg yolks

salt and pepper to taste

1 tablespoon butter

FOR THE CHANTERELLE MUSHROOM BRAISE

6 oz fresh chanterelles- stems cleaned

1 cup demi-glace

1/3 cup vermouth

1 medium shallot, diced fine

1 tablespoon butter

LOBSTER CEVICHE *with Ponzu Sauce*

Most ceviche recipes require you to marinate the raw fish overnight, letting it 'cook' in the citric acid. Unfortunately, the result is usually a rubbery consistency. With this ceviche, you cook the lobster separately (medium rare) and let it cool before preparing the dish. The ponzu sauce adds a citrus soy flavor to the lobster. Shrimp can be substituted for the lobster.

Cook the lobsters for 4-5 minutes in a pot of boiling water. Immediately plunge them in cold water to stop the cooking. When the lobsters are easy to handle, remove the meat from the shells keeping the claw, knuckle and tail meat as intact as possible so when you cut it, the chunks will be uniform. Reserve and keep cold.

MAKE THE PONZU SAUCE
Combine the soy sauce and the vinegar and lemon juice. Reserve.

Cut the lobster into 1/2" pieces. Place the lobster meat in a glass or stainless steel bowl. Add the jalapeños, red onion and the tomatoes. Add the soy/vinegar mixture and toss lightly. Add the olive oil, lime juice and cilantro, tossing again. Taste for salt and pepper.

Place three good looking leaves of the Bibb lettuce on each of the four plates in a star pattern, leaving a space in the center of the plate. Spoon an equal portion of the ceviche onto each lettuce leaf. Mix the daikon and carrots together and pile in the center of each plate. Place a colorful edible flower on the top of the carrot/daikon julienne. Serve immediately. To eat, roll the lettuce leaf with the lobster ceviche like an egg roll.

MISE EN PLACE

2 live Maine lobsters, 1 pound each

12 inner leaves from a head of Boston or Bibb lettuce

1/4 cup Ponzu Sauce (recipe follows)

3 jalapeño chiles, finely diced

1 medium red onion, very thinly sliced

20 teardrop red or cherry tomatoes, cut in half lengthwise

2 tablespoons extra virgin olive oil

2 tablespoons fresh lime juice

1/4 cup cilantro leaves, loosely packed

salt and freshly cracked white pepper

1 tablespoon lemon juice

FOR THE PONZU SAUCE

2 tablespoons light soy sauce

2 tablespoons rice wine vinegar

4 edible flowers, preferably pansies or orchids

1/2 cup daikon, cut into julienne

1/2 cup carrot, cut into julienne

CHILLED DAY BOAT LOBSTER *with Asparagus, Grapefruit, Smoked Peppers and Balsamic-Soy Drizzle*

A very memorable dish. 'Day boat' lobster means lobster caught and delivered that day. Asparagus and grapefruit always go well together (I only use Texas ruby red grapefruit which is optimal during the colder months). The smoked peppers add an unexpected taste.

FOR THE LOBSTER

Place celery, onion and carrots in a large stock pot. Fill halfway with water. Bring to a boil and simmer for twenty minutes. While the water is coming to a boil, skewer the tail of the live lobster so it does not curl when cooking and set up a large bowl two thirds filled with ice water. Plunge the lobster into the boiling water and cook for six minutes. Remove the lobsters and immediately place in the ice water to stop the cooking process. When cool, carefully remove the meat from the tails and claws. Reserve. Do not over-cook the lobsters or the meat will be tough. Reserve and chill, covered with a damp cloth.

FOR THE ASPARAGUS

Blanch the asparagus until just cooked in boiling salted water. Immediately place in ice water and remove when chilled. Reserve at room temperature, covered with a damp paper towel.

ROAST THE RED BELL PEPPERS

Place the red bell peppers over an open flame or under a broiler and blister all sides. Cover in plastic wrap to sweat the pepper. Peel and seed peppers when cool enough to handle. Cut them in a julienne.

FOR THE GRAPEFRUIT

Peel and section the grapefruit making sure that no white rind remains.

FOR THE DRIZZLE

Reduce (separately) the balsamic vinegar and the soy sauce by 1/2. Combine and reserve at room temperature.

ASSEMBLY

Place 3 asparagus randomly on a chilled plate. Slice the lobster tail and arrange over the asparagus. Add the lobster claws around the asparagus. Place 4 sections of grapefruit around the asparagus on each plate. Divide the julienne of red bell pepper onto the top of the lobster tails. Pour 1/4 cup of extra virgin olive oil over and around each plate. Drizzle the balsamic vinegar and soy sauce around the plate - they should bead up in the olive oil. Serve immediately.

MISE EN PLACE

4 live lobsters, 1 pound each

bamboo skewers

Balsamic Soy Drizzle (recipe follows)

12 jumbo asparagus, peeled

2 red bell peppers, blistered, peeled and julienned

2 ruby red grapefruit, peeled, and sectioned

1 celery rib, chopped

1 onion, chopped

1 carrot, chopped

1 cup extra virgin olive oil

FOR THE BALSAMIC SOY DRIZZLE

1/2 cup balsamic vinegar

1/2 cup soy sauce

I prepared this for Julia Child when she was in Dallas, and she loved it. The slow poaching (in olive oil) produces one the best tasting tuna sandwiches ever. The best part is, it doesn't require sushi grade tuna (canned tuna may be used, but only if it's cooked in olive oil).

TO MAKE THE TUNA SALAD

This can be prepared 1 week in advance. The olive oil will keep the submerged tuna fresh for up to 2 weeks when properly refrigerated. Preheat the oven to 275°. In a deep, ovenproof pot, mix the olive oil, herbs, garlic, salt and pepper. Add the tuna, making sure it's completely submerged. Cover with aluminum foil and allow the tuna to cook for 1 hour until tender. Remove from the oven and allow to cool. Place in a storage container and refrigerate. The tuna will stay fresh for up to 3 weeks if properly stored in the refrigerator.

TO MAKE THE MAYONNAISE

Whisk together the egg yolks, mustard and vinegar in a non-reactive bowl. Until thoroughly combined. Slowly trickle in the oil while continuously whisking. The mayonnaise should emulsify and become thick. Season with salt and pepper and chill in a covered container.

TO ASSEMBLE

Remove the tuna from the olive oil and drain well on paper towels. Break the tuna up into medium sized chunks. Season with salt and pepper. Chill. Toast or grill the bread slices. Allow the bread to cool and liberally spread each slice with the mayonnaise. Top two of the slices with the tomatoes, splitting the red and yellow between each. Then add the mesclun. Liberally add the tuna to each stack and top with the other pieces of bread. Slice the sandwich in half and serve with fresh potato chips.

MISE EN PLACE

10 ounces Olive Oil Poached
Tuna Salad (recipe follows)

4 slices from a sourdough boulle

1/4 cup Mayonnaise (recipe follows)

1 ripe red tomato, sliced

1 ripe yellow tomato, sliced

Mesclun

FOR THE TUNA SALAD

1 quart extra virgin olive oil

4 cloves garlic

1 bay leaf

2 sprigs fresh thyme

1 sprig fresh rosemary

10 ounce filet of Big Eye or Yellowfin Tuna

1 teaspoon whole black peppercorns

1 tablespoon salt

FOR THE MAYONNAISE

2 egg yolks

1 teaspoon Dijon mustard

1 1/2 cups vegetable oil

1/2 teaspoon red wine vinegar

salt & pepper to taste

GRILLED SWORDFISH
with ginger/orange crusted oyster and chicory salad

Think of this dish as an asian version of fried oysters (the orange zest and ginger mixed in the bread crumb coating create just the right exotic flavor profile). The vinaigrette is made from a Japanese fruit called yuzu and has a pronounced, tart citrus flavor.

TO MAKE OYSTERS

Mix the panko, orange zest, lemon zest, ginger & parsley together. Dip the oysters in the flour. Shake off the excess flour and dip them in the eggwash. Then roll the oysters in the panko bread crumbs. Fry in 350° oil for 1-2 minutes, until golden brown. Season with salt and pepper and drain on a dry towel. Keep warm.

TO MAKE SWORDFISH

Season the pieces of swordfish with salt & pepper. Brush the fish lightly with oil. Place the swordfish on the grill and cook for 3 minutes per side. The fish should be opaque and not dry looking.

TO MAKE SALAD

Mix all ingredients for the yuzu vinaigrette together and chill. Mix the oysters with 2 tablespoons chicory lettuce and 1 tablespoon shaved fennel. Add the yuzu vinaigrette.

ASSEMBLY

Place the swordfish in the center of plate. Top with the oyster salad and drizzle the kumquat fennel glaze around the plate.

MISE EN PLACE

Ginger/Orange Crusted Oysters (recipe follows)

Grilled Swordfish (recipe follows)

Chicory Salad (recipe follows)

Kumquat Fennel Glaze (see page 92)

Yuzu Vinaigrette

FOR THE OYSTERS

8 shucked oysters (preferably Malpaque Olympia)

1 cup panko (Japanese bread crumbs)

1/2 cup of flour

1/2 cup of eggwash – (2 eggs & 1/2 cup water)

2 teaspoon finely chopped fresh ginger

zest of 1/2 orange

zest of 1/2 lemon

1 tablespoon chopped flat parsley

Yuzu vinaigrette

salt & pepper

FOR THE SWORDFISH

2 pieces of swordfish, 6 ounces each
(3/4" to 1" in thickness)

FOR THE SALAD

2 tablespoons chicory lettuce

1 tablespoon finely shaved fennel

8 ginger/orange crusted oysters

FOR THE YUZU VINAIGRETTE

1/4 vegetable oil

1 tablespoon soy sauce

1 1/2 tablespoon yuzu juice or 1 tablespoon yuzu peelings (available in most Japanese markets)

1 1/2 tablespoons rice wine vinegar

PAN SEARED SCALLOPS

with Red Onion/Jalapeno Marmalade, Applewood Bacon, Studded
Frisee and Extra Virgin Olive Oil

To begin with, you can't go wrong with scallops.(I dearly love them.) The red onion, jalapeño, sugar and balsamic wine reduction is used to create a caramelized effect (that's why I call it 'marmalade'). The salad is a variation of the classic French lardon salad and can be served as either a salad or an entree.

FOR THE JALAPEÑO/ONION JAM

Heat 1 tablespoon of butter in a pan. Place the red onion and jalapeños in the butter and sauté until slightly limp. Add the sugar and cook for 1 more minute. Add two thirds of the balsamic vinegar and cook until all the liquid has evaporated. Season with salt and pepper. Reserve.

FOR THE SALAD

Brown the diced bacon in a pan. Strain the grease and reserve. Mix the frisee, half of the diced shallots and the julienned tomato. Add the rest of the balsamic vinegar and 2 tablespoons extra virgin olive oil. Toss well. Season with salt and pepper.

FOR THE SCALLOPS

Season both sides of the scallops with salt and pepper. In a non-reactive, non-stick pan, heat 1 tablespoon vegetable oil. When the pan begins to lightly smoke, add the scallops. Brown on each side for 2 minutes. Remove from the pan and reserve.

ASSEMBLY

Place the red onion/jalapeño marmalade in the center of each plate. Place equal portions of the frisee salad on top of the marmalade. Place scallops on top of the greens and drizzle the plate with extra olive oil.

INGREDIENTS

12 jumbo sea scallops (preferably dry)

4 jalapeños seeded and julienned

2 red onions, peeled and sliced

4 tablespoons sugar

1/2 cup balsamic vinegar

3 slices of Applewood bacon, finely diced

1 shallot, finely diced

1 tomato, peeled and julienned

1 head of chicory (frisee) curly endive

3 tablespoons extra virgin olive oil

2 tablespoons butter

salt and pepper to taste

SCALLOP *with Lobster Succotash*

Having spent time as a chef in New England, I discovered how popular succotash was, a dish that's prepared mostly for Thanksgiving and Christmas. To make it even more succulent, I added lobster. (What could be more New England than lobster and scallops?)

TO COOK THE LOBSTER

Place a large pot on the stove and add the herbs, wine and water. Bring to a boil and reduce the heat, steeping for 20 minutes at a simmer. Carefully place the lobster in the simmering water and cook for 4-5 minutes. Don't overcook the lobster or it will be tough and chewy. A good measure of doneness is that the shell will have just turned a bright red with some dark blotches. Don't wait for the shell to turn completely red or you will have lobster flavored gum. When cooked, remove the lobster from the pot and immediately place it in ice water to stop the cooking. Remove the lobster meat from the tail and claws. Cut the meat into 1" x 1" pieces. Reserve and refrigerate.

TO MAKE THE SUCCOTASH

Heat the butter in a large sauté pan over medium high heat. When it begins to froth, add the onion, peppers and the shallots. Just as they begin to soften, add the corn and the cream. When the cream has warmed, add the lima beans and haricot vert. Reduce the cream by 1/2 and stir in the cheese. Taste and season with salt and pepper. Remove the lobster meat from the refrigerator and stir it into the succotash. Keep in a warm place.

TO MAKE THE SCALLOPS

Season both sides of the scallops with salt and pepper. Place a non-stick sauté pan over high heat with a little vegetable oil and when the oil begins to smoke, carefully place the scallops in the pan and cook for 1–2 minutes per side or until they are brown on the outside and they have just turned opaque on the inside. Place the cooked scallops on a plate and allow to sit for 1 minute to bleed.

TO ASSEMBLE

Place an equal amount of succotash on the middle of each plate. Place 3 scallops on the center of the succotash. Drizzle with the herb oil and the demi-glace. Garnish each plate with a pinch of micro-sprouts.

MISE EN PLACE

1 - 1 pound lobster

Court Bouillon (recipe follows)

Succotash (recipe follows)

12 jumbo diver scallops

1/4 cup herb oil (optional)

1/4 cup demi-glace, warm (optional)

micro-sprouts

FOR THE COURT BOUILLON

1/2 yellow onion, diced

1/2 carrot, diced

1 rib celery, diced

1 teaspoon black peppercorns

1 bay leaf

1 sprig thyme

1/2 cup white wine

2 quarts water

FOR THE SUCCOTASH

1 tablespoon butter

1/4 red onion diced

1/2 red bell pepper, cleaned and cooked through

1/2 green bell pepper, diced

1/2 teaspoon minced shallots

1 ear corn, kernels removed

1 cup cream

1/2 cup lima beans

2 ounces haricot vert (if unavailable, use small green beans)

2 tablespoons Parmigiano-Reggiano cheese

TEMPURA CRISPED SHRIMP
with Asian Pesto, Roasted Roma Tomatoes and Grilled Eggplant   *Serves 4*

Imagine a light summer fare with a unique presentation – the food in this recipe is stacked dimensionally. I'm convinced nothing is better than tempura batter for frying shrimp (even the moisture from the cooked shrimp will not affect its crunch for at least 20 minutes).

PREPARATION
Preheat oven to 275°. Place the halved tomatoes on a sheet pan. Sprinkle with salt and pepper. Bake for 4-5 hours. The tomatoes should be dry and withered looking.

FOR THE ASIAN PESTO
Place all of the ingredients except for the liquids in a blender. Add half of the olive oil and puree. Slowly add the remaining oil, the sesame oil and the soy sauce. Season to taste; reserve. This can be made 1-2 days in advance.

FOR THE TEMPURA
Place the flour, cornstarch & baking powder in a bowl. Slowly incorporate the cold water until it resembles pancake batter. Season with salt & pepper. Place the canola oil in a pot. Bring to 350°. Dip the shrimp in the tempura batter and lightly place in the hot oil. Move the shrimp around. Cook for 2-3 minutes and remove from oil. Allow the shrimp to drain of excess oil. Reserve and keep warm.

FOR THE EGGPLANT
Heat the grill to medium hot. Grill the eggplant until slightly soft and browned, 1-2 minutes per side; reserve.

ASSEMBLY
Place one slice of eggplant on the center of each plate. Then place 2 halves of roma tomato over the eggplant. Randomly place 3 fried shrimp on top of the tomatoes. Drizzle the Asian Pesto around the plate.

MISE EN PLACE
12 U-15 shrimp, peeled and deveined, tail shell still intact

Tempura Batter (recipe follows)

Asian Pesto (recipe follows)

4 slices eggplant, 1/3" thick

4 roma tomatoes (stemmed and halved)

3 cups canola oil

FOR TEMPURA BATTER
1/2 cup flour

1/2 cup cornstarch

1/8 cup baking powder

1/2 cup cold water

salt and pepper

ASIAN PESTO
1/4 cup mint leaves

1/4 cup basil leaves

1/4 cup cilantro leaves

2 pods garlic

1/4 cup Parmigiano-Reggiano cheese

1/2 extra virgin olive oil

1 teaspoon soy sauce

salt and pepper

This dish is the epitome of summertime (heirloom tomatoes are only in season then). Note the title 'crispy salmon' which you can only achieve by leaving the skin on. Please consider eating the skin, it really is the most flavorful part of the fish.

TO MAKE THE TOMATOES

Cut the stems of the assorted tomatoes; mark an "x" on the bottom of each tomato. Plunge tomatoes in the boiling water until the skin begins to peel back. Immediately place the tomatoes in ice-cold water. Remove tomatoes and peel; reserve.

FOR THE ARTICHOKES

Remove the dark discolored leaves from the artichokes. Cut 1" off the top of the artichoke. Place the artichokes in a pot of boiling water and cook for 20-25 minutes until just tender. (In the restaurant I use vitamin C powder in the water to keep artichokes green in appearance. Remove the artichokes from the water and allow them to drain on a paper towel. Scoop out the hairy chokes and cut artichokes into 4 pieces.

TO MAKE THE BASIL OIL

Place the basil & parsley in a pot of boiling water for 10 seconds, immediately strain the blanched herbs and submerge in ice water. Remove the basil & parsley from the water and squeeze to remove excess water. Place the basil and parsley in a blender with the cup of extra virgin olive oil and blend for 2-3 minutes. Oil will keep for 2-3 days when properly refrigerated.

TO PREPARE THE SALMON FILLETS

Season the fillets with salt and pepper. In a large non-stick pan, place 1 tablespoon extra virgin olive oil. When the oil begins to smoke, add the fish to the pan, skin side down. Cook for 2-3 minutes on the skin side to get the skin crispy. Turn the fish over add the thyme and rosemary to the pan and begin to baste the salmon with the basil oil. Cook for 4 minutes and remove the fish from the pan to a warm plate to rest. The fish should be a perfect medium temperature.

FOR THE ASSEMBLY

Season the peeled tomatoes with salt and pepper, all the tomatoes should be of similar shapes and size. If they are not, you can cut them to obtain a uniform size. Place equal amounts of the heirloom tomatoes on the center of each plate. Place artichoke pieces on plates. Place the salmon fillets skin side facing up on top of the tomatoes. Drizzle the plates with basil oil, balsamic glaze and extra virgin olive oil. Sprinkle the fish with the fresh herbs and serve.

MISE EN PLACE

1 pound of assorted heirloom tomatoes

4 Sterling Salmon Fillets with skin on, 6 ounces each

Basil Oil (recipe follows)

Salmon Fillet (recipe follows)

Balsamic Glaze (page TK)

2 tablespoon basil leaves, roughly chopped

2 large artichokes

FOR THE BASIL OIL

1/2 cup fresh basil leaves only

1/8 cup Italian parsley

1 cup extra virgin olive oil

FOR THE SALMON FILLETS

1 tablespoon extra virgin olive oil

1 sprig each rosemary and thyme

basil oil for basting

LOBSTER FRICASSEE *with Artichokes*

Two food items that blend naturally together – lobster and artichokes. This is a creamy, mild dish where the lobster and artichokes are at center stage.

Trim the stems of the artichokes. In a large steamer basket steam the artichokes until tender about 20 minutes. Let cool.

In a large saucepan, heat 2 1/2 tablespoons of the butter over moderately high heat. Add the pancetta and cook until the fat begins to melt, about 2 minutes. Reduce the heat to moderately low and cook, stirring until the pancetta is browned about 7 minutes longer. Add the onion, carrots, parsley sprigs and cook, stirring occasionally until the onion is soft, about 10 minutes.

Meanwhile, remove the artichokes and scoop out the hairy chokes. Cut the bottoms in 1" wedges and add to the onion and carrot mixture with 1 cup of water. Bring to a simmer over moderate heat and cook until the carrots are tender, about 10 minutes longer.

Strain and reserve the vegetables and liquid separately, discard the parsley sprigs. Set the liquid aside for 10 minutes, then skim off as much fat as possible from the surface. Pour the liquid into medium non-reactive saucepan and add the lemon juice. Boil over moderately high heat until it has reduced to 1/2 cup, about 5 minutes. Add the 1/2 cup of cream and reduce by two thirds. Reduce the heat to low and whisk in the remaining stick of butter, 1 tablespoon at a time until it is thoroughly incorporated and the sauce is creamy.

Add the reserved vegetables, the lobster meat, minced parsley and tarragon. Season to taste with salt and pepper, warm just until heated through. Serve immediately.

INGREDIENTS

4 large artichokes

1 stick plus 2 tablespoons cold unsalted butter, cut in tablespoon-size bits

2 ounces pancetta, minced-or applewood bacon

1/2 cup heavy cream

1 large onion halved lengthwise and thinly sliced

2 medium carrots thinly sliced

2 parsley sprigs plus 1 tablespoon minced parsley

2 tablespoons fresh lemon juice

2 boiled lobsters, 1 pound each, meat removed and cut in 1" chunks

1 tablespoon chopped fresh tarragon

salt and freshly ground pepper

Once in a while, a presentation is interesting enough to be fun, and doesn't have to add flavor. For example, in this dish we use sugar cane as a skewer. It's a visual 'trick' that looks great at the table. (It helps to have a wok to make great stir fry, but if unavailable, a large heavy duty sauté pan will do.)

TO COOK AND PREPARE TUNA WITH THE SUGAR CANE

Preheat a grill or heat up a large sauté pan. If the sugar cane is more than 1/2" in diameter, cut it 1/2 lengthwise. Skewer through the middle of the tuna with one piece of sugar cane. Season the tuna with salt & pepper. Add one tablespoon vegetable oil to hot sauté pan. Place the tuna in the pan and cook on high heat for 1-2 minutes per side for rare tuna. If you are grilling it, cook the tuna for the same amount of time on the flame grill. Remove tuna and allow it to rest on a plate until the stir-fry is complete.

TO MAKE STIR FRY VEGETABLES

Heat a wok or a large sauté pan. Add 1 tablespoon vegetable oil to the pan and heat until it begins to smoke. Add the vegetables and sauté for 15 seconds. Add the garlic, ginger, soy sauce and oyster sauce and bring to a boil. Add the cornstarch and water mixture (called 'slurry') to the oyster and soy sauce. The sauce will immediately thicken; if it becomes too thick you can add water to thin.

ASSEMBLY

Ladle the oyster/soy sauce with the vegetables into a bowl. Place the tuna on top of the vegetables and serve.

MISE EN PLACE

Tuna on Sugar Cane skewers

1 recipe of Stir-Fried Vegetables (recipe follows)

FOR THE TUNA

4 portions sushi grade tuna, 6 ounces each and cut in a filet

4 sugarcane skewers

1 teaspoon vegetable oil

salt and pepper

FOR THE STIR-FRY

1 teaspoon vegetable oil

8 ears of baby corn

8 baby carrots, peeled, with tops left intact

1 head of Chinese Choy sum or baby Bok Choy

1 teaspoon chopped ginger

2 scallions – cut on a bias

1/4 cup of soy sauce

1/4 oyster sauce (available in Asian markets)

1/2 teaspoon chopped garlic

2 teaspoons cornstarch and 2 1/2 teaspoons warm water, mixed together

1/2 teaspoon sesame oil

1 teaspoon vegetable oil

SUSHI

"During the trip to Tokyo we ate sushi almost every meal — including dining at Kyubei, the most expensive restaurant in the city — but nothing surpassed the sushi I had at the stall in the fish market."

Citizen is a restaurant born of many influences. When we first started thinking exactly what kind of restaurant it would be, we had a somewhat vague idea that the restaurant would combine the best of European (specifically French) cooking techniques with the best of Asian ingredients. It took a trip to New York to really push us down that path. We visited Nobu, an incredible restaurant in Tribeca. Nobu, whose first restaurant was in L.A., single-handedly pioneered this overall idea (that East can meet West in the kitchen).

Shortly after that trip, we decided to take the plunge and go to Tokyo. We wanted to make sure that we had researched all aspects of opening a totally new concept.

The very first restaurant I visited in Tokyo was a sushi 'stall' (there is no other way to describe it.) It was literally at the fish market, a tiny place that sat maybe six people. Immaculately clean (as you might suspect) with the owners giving full attention to the patrons.

To my surprise, the sushi blew me away. Every taste was clean, crisp and wonderful. During the trip we ate sushi almost every meal — including at the most expensive sushi restaurant in the city, Kyubei — but nothing surpassed the sushi I consumed at the stall in the fish market.

The trip changed our entire thinking. Before, we weren't sure what role sushi would play. We knew we were going to offer it, but now we knew sushi had to take a very prominent role at Citizen. That meant making a commitment to hire an authentic Japanese sushi chef (say hello to Yutaka when you're there).

TUNA SASHIMI

Slice the Tuna as thinly as possible about 1/8th inch thickness. Line four plates with the four Bamboo leaves. Place equal amounts of julienne daikon on top of the Bamboo leaves. Place the Tuna around the julienne daikon. Place a lemon semi circle next to the tuna. Divide the lite soy sauce and Wasabi into 4 small side plates or bowls.

INGREDIENTS

4 tuna filets (big eye or blue fin), 3 ounces each

4 shiso leaves

4 ounce julienne daikon

4 bamboo leaves

4 thin slices of lemon - cut in semi circle

4 ounces lite soy sauce

2 tablespoons wasabi

SHRIMP TEMPURA ROLL

This is a favorite roll at Citizen. It blends the crispy, chrunchiness of tempura with creamy avocado.

Fry the Tempura Shrimp – see recipe

TO SPREAD THE RICE

Place 1/4 cup of vinegared rice 1/8 inch thickness on 1/2 sheet of Nori. Spread the rice out to the end of the Nori Sheet. Using your finger run a small streak of Wasabi through the middle of the rice. Then spread 1/2 tablespoon of flying fish roe over the wasabi. Then place the fried Tempura shrimp over the flying fish roe. Slice the avocado in thin strips and place over the shrimp.

TO ROLL:

Lift the end of the Nori closest to you and roll it over the filling, pressing down as you roll. When rolled it should feel like a firm cigar. Cut each roll in 6 to 8 pieces.

INGREDIENTS

1 cup prepared vinegar rice

2 sheets of dried nori cut in half

4 jumbo shrimp tempura fried (see Recipe)

1/2 avocado, peeled and sliced

1 tablespoon flying fish roe (Tobiko)

1 teaspoon of prepared wasabi

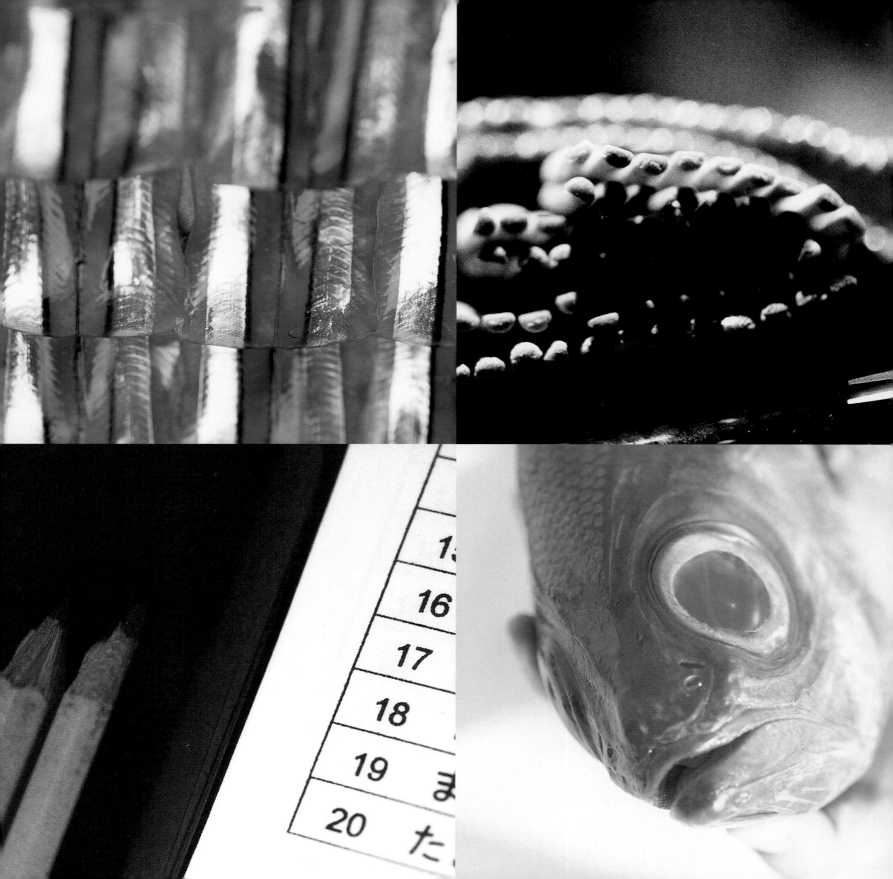

TO FORM THE SUSHI

With one finger, press the vinegared rice into a fairly firm oval in the palm of your opposite hand. This Sushi Rice that has been formed should resemble a tapered wine cork. Place 1/4 teaspoon of the Wasabi on the top of the rice and gently mold the salmon to the rice.

Serve with equal parts of soy sauce and the remaining tablespoon of Wasabi for dipping.

INGREDIENTS

8 salmon slices, 1/8 inch thick

2/3 cup vinegared rice- see recipe

1 tablespoon and 1 teaspoon wasabi

1/4 cup lite soy sauce

SUSHI RICE

Makes 1 gallon

TO COOK THE RICE/ USING A RICE COOKER

Place the rice in a large bowl and run under cold water, rub the rice with your hands and change the water until the water turns clear from cloudy.

Add the 5 cups of water to the 5 cups of rice and place in a rice cooker. When the water is completely absorbed, turn off the cooker and let the rice rest for 15 minutes. Remove the cooked rice from the cooker and place in a wooden bowl. Pour the vinegar dressing all over the rice. Quickly mix the dressing into the rice. Allow this to cool to room temperature. You need to keep the rice at room temperature until ready to use.

INGREDIENTS

5 cups short grain rice

5 cups water

FOR THE DRESSING

1 cup rice wine vinegar-seaweed

1 Sheet of konbu, 2"

1/4 cup of sugar

MEATS

"There is obviously nothing wrong with prime beef, but at least once in your life, you have to try Kobe beef. Its extensive marbling produces a texture that is literally butter-like."

I am asked this frequently. People want to know how I like my own steak cooked. I believe most chefs will give the same answer – rare. But when they ask what the best cut of beef is, I say "anything Kobe," which usually surprises them. There is obviously nothing wrong with prime beef, but at least once in your life, you have to try Kobe beef. Its extensive marbling produces a texture that is literally butter-like. I know it's expensive. I'm just saying, try it once in your lifetime.

Another question I'm often asked (and I'm happy to answer) is how to grill a steak. Is there a best way? I think so. Whether you grill your steak (I prefer wood or charcoal) or sauté it, you should turn the steak only three times once you've placed it on the grill (or in the pan). Your goal is to cook it roughly 1/4 of the way to your preference (medium, medium rare, etc.) before you make the first turn, and then cook it another 1/4 of the way after each subsequent turn. So once your steak is on the grill, your first turn will be to simply turn it over. On your second turn, however, turn the steak 90° to the original alignment. The last turn is just to turn the steak over again (keeping it 90° to the original alignment). This sounds more complicated than it is, but it will put those wonderful 'X' marks on your steaks. Another hint: take your steak off the grill before it's finished cooking the way you like it, and let it 'rest' for 10 to 15 minutes. It will continue to cook from the heated juices inside and will eliminate the 'bleeding' you see with steaks.

We also serve a lot of lamb at my restaurants. Don't overlook the shanks. It's amazing what two to three hours will do when you're braising a lamb shank. (As a note, we only use domestic lamb. It has a milder, 'cleaner' flavor.) In all of the recipes where bacon is used, I only use applewood smoked bacon. There is no substitute for this heavenly product.

CITRUS BEEF

This is a dish that is best made in a wok (a cast iron wok – such as Le Creuset – would probably work best). One of my most popular dishes at Citizen, this is a variation of tangerine beef (feel free to use the peels from all citrus fruit including grapefruit and lemon.)

TO MAKE THE SAUCE

Heat a large pot or wok until it is very hot. Add the oil, and when it begins to smoke add the Szechuan chiles, ginger, garlic, vinegar and sugar. Cook this mixture down until it becomes syrupy and bubbly. Add the orange juice and reduce by 1/2. While the sauce is cooking down, take a paring knife and cut off the peel of an orange. Remove any white pith from the peels and roughly cut into pieces about the size of a quarter. When the sauce has reduced, stir in the peel, soy sauce, hoisin sauce, ketchup and sesame oil. Bring to a boil again, and remove from the heat. Strain through a fine strainer and reserve. This may be done up to a day ahead.

TO MAKE THE BEEF

Mix the flour and water into a paste. Toss the beef in the flour paste. This step may be done a day ahead if the beef is kept refrigerated and submerged in the paste. When you are ready to cook, heat the oil in the wok to 400°. Remove each slice of the beef from the paste. At this point they will be pasty and goopy. That's okay. Dredge the coated beef slices in the potato flour and shake off the excess. Fry the beef until a golden brown crust forms. Remove from the oil and drain on paper towels. Pour off all but two tablespoons of the hot oil. Skim off any crumbs from the oil.

TO FINISH AND ASSEMBLE

Heat the oil until it begins to smoke. Toss the broccoli and fried beef into the wok and begin to stir-fry using a scooping motion with a Chinese spatula. The food in the wok should be constantly moving. Add enough of the Orange Sauce to coat the meat and broccoli. Toss in the grated ginger and sesame oil. This stir-fry process should take less than a minute. Scoop onto a serving dish and sprinkle with the sliced scallions. Serve immediately.

MISE EN PLACE

8 ounces Orange Sauce

1/4 cup flour

1/2 cup water

1 pound flank steak sliced on a diagonal, 1/8" thick

2 cups potato flour

3 cups peanut oil

1/2 cup cut broccoli florets – lightly blanched

1/2 teaspoon fresh grated ginger

1/4 teaspoon sesame oil

1/4 cup scallions, cut 1/4" thick

FOR THE ORANGE SAUCE

2 tablespoons vegetable oil

3 szechuan chile peppers

1 teaspoon chopped ginger

1/2 cup rice wine vinegar

1/2 cup sugar

1 cup fresh orange juice

2 oranges

1/2 cup soy sauce, regular or light

1/2 cup hoisin sauce

1/2 cup ketchup

1/2 teaspoon sesame oil

With this dish, the sauce is the focus. The picante balsamic flavor will add a sweet-sour taste with a syrupy consistency. The use of demi-glace is not essential for the completion of this dish.

TO MAKE BEEF TENDERLOIN

Broil beef tenderloin to desired degree of doneness, about 3 minutes each side for medium rare. Remove from heat and keep warm. Remember, turn the beef 3 times.

TO MAKE PIQUANT BALSAMIC SAUCE

In a large saucepan over medium high heat, combine sliced apples, shallots, thyme, port, red wine, and balsamic vinegar. Reduce the liquids by two thirds. Add the demi-glace and reduce until the sauce coats the back of a spoon. Strain through a fine strainer. Swirl the 2 tablespoons butter into the sauce to smooth out its taste. Add the lime juice. Season to taste.

MISE EN PLACE

Cooking procedure for beef tenderloin

Piquant Balsamic Sauce (recipe follows)

FOR BEEF TENDERLOIN

4, 8 ounces each center cut beef tenderloin

FOR PIQUANT BALSAMIC SAUCE

1 red delicious apple, cored and sliced thin

1 granny smith apple, cored and sliced thin

1 shallot, finely chopped

2 sprigs fresh thyme

1/4 cup port wine

1/2 cup red wine

1/2 cup demi-glace

1/4 cup balsamic vinegar

2 tablespoons very cold butter

juice of 1 lime

salt and pepper

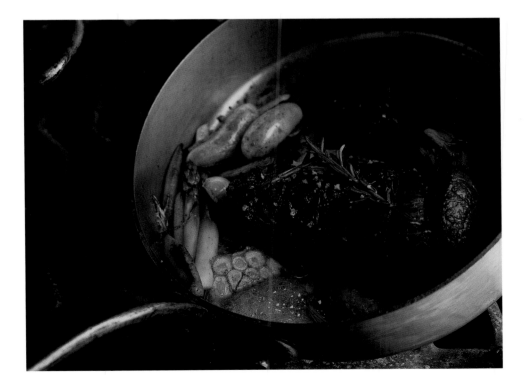

What makes a rib-eye a cowboy rib-eye? The cut of meat. A cowboy rib-eye is a large rib eye steak with the bone still attached. The bone adds flavor. The buttermilk onion rings add a touch of nostalgia.

TO MAKE THE ONION RINGS

Peel the onion and slice in 1/2" to 3/4" thick slices. Separate the inner rings of the onion slices. Carefully remove the thin inner skin of each of the rings. Mix all of the above ingredients in a bowl except for the flour. Lightly sprinkle the bare onion rings with water. Then place the rings into the flour. Shake off the excess flour and then dip the rings into the buttermilk mixture. Remove the rings from the buttermilk and redip into the flour. Shake off the excess flour and reserve on a sheet pan. In a large pan or electric fryer heat up the oil to 350°. Place half of the rings into the hot oil and cook until golden brown. Do not cook all of the rings together to avoid lowering the oil temperature too much. When the onion rings are golden and crispy carefully remove them from the oil and allow to drain on a dry towel. Sprinkle with salt and reserve in a warm place.

COOKING THE STEAKS

Preheat an outdoor grill with your favorite wood, charcoal or other grilling method. Season both sides of the steaks with salt and pepper. Lightly brush steaks with 2 tablespoons of vegetable oil. Place the steaks on the grill and cook on each side for 4-5 minutes for medium rare. Remove the steaks from the grill and place them on a platter to "rest" for 10 minutes. Resting the meat will enable it to cook equally through and prevent it from bleeding on your plate.

TO SERVE

Place the steaks on a large plate. Pile the onion rings on top of the steak, place the watercress salad on top of the onion rings.

MISE EN PLACE

2 bone-in rib-eye steaks, 18-20 ounce each

20 Buttermilk Onion Rings (recipe follows)

2 cups Watercress Salad (recipe follows)

FOR THE ONION RINGS

1 large spanish onion

1 cup buttermilk

1 cup water

2 eggs

2 teaspoons cayenne pepper

1 tablespoon salt

2 teaspoons table grind black pepper

1 teaspoon paprika

1/2 teaspoon cumin

2 cups of all-purpose flour

FOR THE WATERCRESS SALAD

2 bunches fresh watercress

1 teaspoon finely diced shallots

1 tablespoon diced tomato concassé

2 tablespoons balsamic vinaigrette

GRILLED COLORADO LAMB CHOP
with Roquefort Flan and Cumin Scented Lamb Jus

Serves 8

For this dish, please only use what I use – domestic lamb from Colorado. It has a wonderful mild, clean flavor. This single chop is served with a roquefort flan (roquefort and lamb blend well with each other). Cumin replaces the more expected rosemary or thyme.

TO MAKE THE FLAN
Preheat the oven to 375°. Split each head of garlic and roast in a small pan until lightly browned, about 40 minutes. When the garlic is done, reduce the heat in the oven to 300°. Oil the ramekins. Whisk together 2 yolks and 1 egg in a bowl. Squeeze the garlic into the cream in a small pot and bring to a boil. Remove from the fire and add the Roquefort. Let infuse for 5-10 minutes. Pass through a fine strainer. Pour the flan base into the oiled ramekins. Place the filled ramekins in a water bath and cook for 25-30 minutes or until just set. Remove from the oven and allow to rest. Keep warm.

TO MAKE THE LAMB JUS
Preheat the oven to 450°. Roast the reserved lamb scraps until browned in a heavy gauge pan. Remove from the oven and drain off the grease. Return the browned scraps to the pan and add the onion, celery, shallot and garlic. Saute until all of the vegetables have browned. Deglaze with the wine and reduce by two thirds. Add the demi-glace and reduce the sauce until it coats the back of a spoon. Add the cumin and simmer for five minutes more and pass through a fine strainer. Reserve and keep warm.

FOR THE CHOPS
Preheat a grill. Slice the lamb into 8 chops. Season each chop with salt and pepper and brush with the oil. Sear the lamb chops on the grill, cooking 2-3 minutes on each side for medium rare. Remove from the grill and let rest for 5 minutes.

TO ASSEMBLE
Invert a warm flan onto each plate. Place 2 chops on either side of the flan and spoon a little of the sauce next to each chop. Toss the mesclun with the vinaigrette and place 1/2 cup between the chops. Serve.

MISE EN PLACE
4 Roquefort Flans (recipe follows)

8 Lamb chops (recipe follows)

1 cup Lamb Jus (recipe follows)

2 cups mesclun

3 tablespoons Champagne Vinaigrette (see page 50)

FOR THE ROQUEFORT FLANS
2 heads garlic

1 egg

2 egg yolks

1 cup heavy cream

2 ounces Roquefort cheese, crumbled

salt and freshly ground black pepper

4, 2 ounces each aluminum molds or ramekins

FOR THE LAMB CHOPS
1 domestic rack of lamb, cleaned and frenched, trimmings reserved

salt and pepper

2 tablespoons extra virgin olive oil

FOR THE CUMIN LAMB JUS
Trimmings from the rack of lamb

1/4 cup chopped yellow onion

1/4 cup chopped celery

1 shallot, sliced

4 cloves garlic, chopped

1/2 cup white wine

1 1/2 cups demi-glace

1 teaspoon ground cumin

MEATS 125

CORIANDER CRUSTED VENISON LOIN
with a Duck Confit Pancake, Wilted Watercress
and Pomegranate and Pepper Hunter Sauce

A health conscious dish. Not many know that venison is very lean and low in cholesterol.
The coriander rub adds a clean and pungent flavor to the venison loin.

TO PREP THE PANCAKE

Place the potatoes in a pot with water to cover and cook until tender, about 15-20 minutes. Place the potatoes in a ricer or finely mash. Season with salt and pepper to taste. Add the cut up duck confit, chives and egg yolk. Portion the mix into 4, 3 " thick pancakes with your hands, cover with waxed paper and reserve in the refrigerator. They may be kept in the refrigerator for up to 1 day.

TO MAKE THE CORIANDER CRUST

Toast the coriander seeds until lightly browned in a small sauté pan. Do this over high heat, tossing the seeds in the pan until they become fragrant and lightly toasted. Immediately place in a coffee grinder and grind up finely. Add the pepper, parsley, sugar and salt and lightly grind. Pat the coriander rub on the loin and reserve.

TO MAKE THE SAUCE

In a saucepan, heat the oil until it smokes and add the onion and celery. Sauté until lightly browned. Add the cracked pepper and currant jelly. Deglaze with the white wine and reduce by half. Add the demi-glace and vinegar, and cook over high heat until desired consistency is reached. Season with salt and pepper to taste and strain. Reserve in a warm place.

TO FINISH THE PANCAKES

Heat a non-stick pan over medium heat. Place the pancakes in the pan and lightly brown on both sides, using no oil. Reserve and keep warm.

TO COOK THE VENISON

Preheat oven to 400°. In an ovenproof sauté pan, heat the oil over high heat and sear the venison on all sides. Roast the venison in the oven for 10-15 minutes (for medium rare). Remove from pan and allow to bleed. Keep warm.

TO MAKE WILTED WATERCRESS AND ASSEMBLE

Place the duck pancake in the middle of each of 4 serving plates. Slice the venison equally into 8 medallion size portions. Overlap 2 slices of venison on top of the pota-

continued on next page ➤

MISE EN PLACE

Coriander Crust (recipe follows)

20 ounces venison loin

2 tablespoons extra virgin olive oil

Duck Confit Pancake (recipe follows)

Pepper Hunter Sauce (recipe follows)

Wilted Watercress (recipe follows)

2 tablespoons extra virgin olive oil

1 medium shallot, minced

1 pomegranate, seeds removed and reserved

FOR THE DUCK CONFIT PANCAKE

2 potatoes (peeled and roughly cut)

1 recipe Duck Confit (see page 71), torn into bite-size pieces

2 teaspoon finely minced chives

1 egg yolk

FOR THE CORIANDER CRUST

1 tablespoon toasted coriander seeds

1 teaspoon cracked white pepper

2 teaspoon chopped parsley

1 teaspoon sugar

1/2 teaspoon salt

FOR THE HUNTER SAUCE

1 tablespoon extra virgin olive oil

1/2 medium yellow onion, diced

1/2 celery stalk, ribbed and diced

1 teaspoon cracked black pepper

1 tablespoon currant jelly

1/2 cup white wine

continued on next page ➤

to. Keep warm in a very slow oven.

In a very hot sauté pan, add the diced shallots and the watercress. Sauté until the watercress is slightly wilted. Season with salt and pepper. Place the watercress directly on top of the venison. Drizzle the sauce around the plate and sprinkle the pomegranate seeds around the plate. Serve immediately.

1 cup demi-glace (see page 25)

1 tablespoon red wine vinegar

FOR THE WILTED WATERCRESS

3 heads watercress

1 tablespoon olive oil

1 medium shallot, minced

Salsify? It's an under appreciated vegetable that resembles white asparagus and has a milder taste. For this dish, the marinated double cut pork chops are grilled and placed on a silky risotto.

TO MAKE THE SAUCE

Place 1 tablespoon of butter in a small pan. When the butter begins to brown add the shallots and garlic. Sauté until shallots and garlic begin to brown. Add the white wine, the red wine vinegar (deglaze) and reduce by two thirds. Add the cracked pepper and demi-glace. Reduce the sauce until it coats the back of a spoon. Season with salt and strain the sauce, keep in a warm place.

TO MAKE SALSIFY/ASPARAGUS RISOTTO

In a non-stick pan heat 1 tablespoon unsalted butter. When butter begins to brown add the risotto and lightly sauté. Add 1/2 of vegetable or chicken stock. Incorporate the stock vigorously, you want to stir the risotto as much as possible to release the starch. The risotto should take on a creamy appearance although no cream is used. Add the sliced asparagus and salsify. Add the parmesan cheese and continue to stir. Add the rest of the stock and the other tablespoon butter. Season with salt and pepper. Fold in the tomato concassé and chives. I prefer risotto to be somewhat loose and runny with a very creamy appearance. You can adjust the amount of stock you use to meet your preference.

TO MAKE PORK MARINADE

Bring all of the ingredients to a boil. Let the mixture simmer for 30 minutes until it comes to a syrup like consistency. Chill. This can be used for basting, chicken and steaks.

TO COOK THE PORK CHOPS

Preheat a grill. Season the chops with salt and pepper. Place the double cut chops on the grill and cook for 10-15 minutes on each side for medium doneness. During the last 5 minutes of cooking, brush one side of the pork with the mustard. Remove from the grill and let the meat rest for 10 minutes before serving.

ASSEMBLY

Place the creamy salsify / asparagus risotto in the center of the plate. Place the double cut pork chop with the Dijon mustard glazed side up on top of the risotto. Drizzle the sauce around the risotto.

MISE EN PLACE

4 thick pork chops, 1 1/2"-2" thick

Salsify/asparagus risotto (recipe follows)

Pork Marinade (recipe follows)

Sauce (recipe follows)

FOR THE SAUCE

3 tablespoons chopped shallots

1 teaspoon chopped garlic

1/2 cup white wine

1/4 cup good red wine vinegar

1 tablespoon cracked black pepper

1 tablespoon unsalted butter

1 cup demi-glace

FOR THE SALSIFY/ASPARAGUS RISOTTO

8 asparagus peeled, cooked and cut into small bias slices

2 pieces salsify – peeled, cooked and cut into small bias shapes

1 cup risotto, already 2/3rds cooked following instructions for a basic risotto in Lemon Risotto, page 159)

1 cup vegetable or chicken stock

1/2 cup Parmigiano-Reggiano

2 tablespoons tomato concassé

1 tablespoon chopped fine chives

2 tablespoons butter

salt and pepper

FOR PORK MARINADE

3 cups of water

1/2 cup brown sugar

1/4 cup honey

4 cloves garlic

1 teaspoon mustard seed

1/2 cup light soy sauce

1 medium onion sliced

2 sprigs of rosemary

1 bay leaf

1 teaspoon whole black peppercorn

GRILLED RARE TENDERLOIN *with Chilled Sweet*
Vermicelli, Spicy Cucumbers and Soy/Mirin Sauce

This can also work as a cold appetizer – the subtle asian flavors elevates the tenderloin in an unexpected direction. Tuna can be substituted for beef.

TO MAKE THE VERMICELLI

Cook the angel-hair pasta in boiling salted water until al dente. Strain and cool under cold running water. Drain completely. Lightly toss with the sweet and sour sauce and the sliced scallions. Reserve and refrigerate.

TO MAKE THE CUCUMBERS

Toss the julienne of cucumber with the sambal and season to taste with salt and pepper. Reserve and refrigerate.

TO MAKE THE SOY/MIRIN SAUCE

Combine the soy sauce, rice wine vinegar, mirin, sesame oil and chopped garlic. Reserve.

TO MAKE THE BEEF TENDERLOIN

Season the beef with salt and pepper. Either grill or sauté the beef until very rare, 2 minutes per side over very high heat. Let the tenderloin rest for about 3 minutes, allowing it to bleed. Slice the tenderloin thinly against the grain and toss with 1/4 of the soy/mirin sauce. Reserve.

TO ASSEMBLE

Divide the tossed vermicelli into 4 portions and place in the middle of each of four serving plates. Do the same with the sliced tenderloin, placing over the top of the vermicelli. Place the julienned cucumber over the sliced beef and put a small pinch of the pickled ginger on top of the cucumbers. Spoon the soy/mirin sauce around the angel-hair pasta. Serve immediately.

*European or English cucumber is more uniform in shape; the seeds are very small.

MISE EN PLACE

Vermicelli

1 european cucumber*, peeled and seeded, thinly sliced lengthwise and cut into a julienne

2 tablespoons sambal (oriental chili paste, available in Asian markets)

Cooked tenderloin

Soy/Mirin Sauce (recipe follows)

FOR THE VERMICELLI

2 cups angel-hair pasta

2 tablespoons sweet and sour sauce (available in Asian markets)

2 tablespoons sliced scallions, cut thinly on the diagonal

FOR THE SOY/MIRIN SAUCE

1/2 cup soy sauce

1/4 cup rice wine vinegar

2 tablespoons mirin

1/2 teaspoon sesame oil

1 teaspoon chopped garlic

8 ounces beef tenderloin

salt and pepper

1/4 cup pickled ginger

A word of caution: frying pork for this dish requires a pot that can stand being heated to 375°. Just be careful. This recipe is simplicity in itself. Salt. Pepper. Sugar. Some peppers and cilantro at the end.

TO PRE-COOK PORK

Place the julienne of pork in the potato flour, shaking off any excess. Fry the pork in 2 quarts of peanut oil heated to 375° in a heavy pot or wok until very lightly browned, about 1-1 1/2 minutes. Strain the pork and drain on paper towels. Reserve 2 tablespoons of the oil.

TO MAKE THE PANCAKE

Preheat oven to 200°. Place the rice pancakes in a warm oven until they become pliable. Brush the pancakes with a light layer of plum sauce. Fold the rice pancakes in half, and fold in half once more. Keep warm.

TO FINISH THE PORK AND ASSEMBLE

Heat wok or a sauté pan until extremely hot and add 2 tablespoons of oil. When the oil begins to smoke, quickly add the pre-cooked pork strips. Toss the pork for 20-30 seconds, season with salt and pepper and sprinkle the sugar over the pork while tossing. Add the serrano peppers, garlic, soy sauce and sesame oil. Just before removing from the stove, add the cilantro and scallions. Toss briefly. Serve on the center of each plate with the plum rice pancake resting on the rim of the dish.

This should be a dry looking dish. There is no sauce to speak of.

INGREDIENTS

14 ounces pork loin, sliced into 1/4" strips on the diagonal

6 ounces potato flour

2 quarts peanut oil

salt and freshly ground black pepper

1 teaspoon granulated sugar

3 green serrano chile peppers, seeded and julienned

1/2 teaspoon chopped garlic

2 tablespoons soy sauce

1/2 teaspoon sesame oil

1/4 cup cilantro leaves, loosely packed

2 tablespoons sliced scallions, cut on the bias

8 rice pancakes

4 ounces plum sauce (available at most Asian markets)

TENDERLOIN OF BEEF WITH BRAISED SHORT RIBS,
Béarnaise Sauce, Mousseline Potatoes and Baby Arugula Salad

Serves 4

Braising short ribs is a very basic technique and also very luxurious cooking. Turning an average cut of meat into a succulent mouth watering dish in 2 to 3 hours is exhilarating. The béarnaise sauce is a throwback to my earlier years of cooking.

TO MAKE THE SHORT RIBS

Preheat oven to 450°. Season the short ribs with salt and pepper. Heat the vegetable oil in a large oven-proof sauté pan. Add the short ribs and brown on all sides. Add the diced vegetables and continue to cook until they are lightly browned. Deglaze the pan with the water, scraping the bits from the bottom of the pan. Add the demi-glace, bring to a simmer, cover the pan and braise for 1-1/2 hours or until the meat almost comes off of the bone. Remove the cooked short ribs from the pan. Reserve and keep warm. Strain and skim the oil from the sauce. Season the sauce to taste; reserve and keep warm.

MISE EN PLACE

Short Ribs (recipe follows)

Béarnaise Sauce (recipe follows)

Baby Arugula Salad (recipe follows)

Potato Purée (recipe follows)

4 filets of beef, 6 ounces each

salt and freshly ground black pepper

FOR THE SHORT RIBS

4 short ribs, 4" thick

1/2 carrot, peeled and diced

TO MAKE THE POTATOES

Peel the potatoes, submerge into salted water and boil for 25 minutes or until tender. While the potatoes are boiling, bring the horseradish and cream to a boil. Remove from the heat and purée in a blender. Set aside. Strain the cooked potatoes. Put the potatoes and butter in a ricer and process through. Add 1/2 to 1 cup cream to the buttered potatoes. Season with salt and pepper and keep warm. These should be very rich and luxurious. Add the blended horseradish cream to the potatoes. Keep warm, covering the pot with a towel. For super-smooth potatoes pass them through a chinois.

TO MAKE THE BEARNAISE SAUCE

Place the shallots, vinegar and tarragon in a pan and reduce until the liquid has all but evaporated. The tarragon reduction will be very pungent. Put the egg yolks in a stainless steel bowl, place over a pot of simmering water and whip until the yolks are thick and lemon yellow in color. Remove from the heat. Slowly drizzle the clarified butter into the yolks. The more butter you add the thicker the sauce will become. Add the tarragon reduction and chopped parsley. Season with salt and pepper to taste. Keep in a slightly warm place until ready.

TO MAKE BABY ARUGULA SALAD

Slice the shallots into thin rings. Sprinkle with water. Dust with flour and fry in 350° oil until golden brown. Remove the shallots from the oil and drain on a dry towel. Toss with the baby arugula and balsamic vinaigrette.

TO MAKE THE FILETS

Preheat the grill. Season the steaks with salt and pepper. Brush with vegetable oil and cook on each side for 7-8 minutes for medium rare. Remove from the grill and let the meat rest for 10 minutes.

TO ASSEMBLE

Spoon out a dollop of horseradish potatoes on a plate. Place the short rib on top of the horseradish potatoes. Place the grilled filet next to the short rib. Spoon a generous portion of Bearnaise sauce over the filet. Serve immediately.

1/2 medium yellow onion, diced

1 rib celery, diced

1 cup demi-glace

2 cups vegetable stock or water

1 sprig thyme

1 bay leaf

salt and freshly ground black pepper

FOR THE POTATO PURÉE

2 tablespoons grated fresh horseradish

1/2 cup heavy cream

1 1/2 pound Yukon Gold potatoes, peeled and quartered

1 cup cream

1 pound unsalted butter

FOR THE BÉARNAISE SAUCE

3 egg yolks

1 pound unsalted butter, clarified

1/2 teaspoon shallots, chopped

1 tablespoon chopped parsley

1 cup red wine vinegar

2 tablespoons dried tarragon

FOR THE BABY ARUGULA SALAD

1 cup baby arugula

1 tablespoon balsamic vinaigrette

3/4 cup sliced shallots

1/2 cup flour

2 cups vegetable oil for frying

VEAL CHOP *with Vegetable Spring Rolls and Mirin Sauce*

I love when European cooking and Asia ingredients collide. Here the classic European veal chop is served over 2 spring rolls with a sweet rice wine sauce (aka mirin).

TO PREP THE VEGETABLES

Cook the corn, asparagus, carrots and broccoli in simmering water just until tender. Shock the vegetables in cold water to stop the cooking. Reserve.

TO MAKE SPRING ROLLS

Heat 1 tablespoon of the oil in a skillet or wok over high heat. When the oil begins to smoke, add the cabbage and sauté until soft. Add the garlic and soy sauce; cook until all the liquid has all but evaporated. Season to taste with salt and pepper. Place the cabbage in a strainer to discard any liquid that may bleed out. Repeat this process with the shiitake mushrooms. Reserve and chill both ingredients by placing the strainer in a bowl and cover.

TO ASSEMBLE THE SPRING ROLLS

Place a spring roll wrapper on a table with a pointed corner facing you. Place on wraper, 1" inch in from the corner facing you: 1/2 teaspoon shiitake, 1 teaspoon cabbage, a little carrot and a little of the cooked angel-hair pasta. You do not want to have too much filling. When rolled the rolls should resemble a short, fat cigar. Begin to roll up the spring roll, halfway up the spring roll while rolling fold in the sides and continue to tightly roll up the spring roll. When the roll comes up almost to other corner of the wrapper, brush a little egg onto the corner and seal. Reserve. These may be made 1-2 days in advance. Store in the refrigerator, tightly covered with plastic wrap.

TO MAKE THE MIRIN SAUCE

Heat 1 teaspoon of the oil in a saucepan or wok over high heat. When it begins to smoke add the shallots, garlic and lemon grass; cook for 2-3 minutes. Then add the mirin and vinegar. Reduce by 1/2. Add the demi-glace, turn the heat down and simmer for 20 minutes. Be sure to skim the impurities that have risen to the top of the sauce. Continue to cook until the sauce coats the back of a spoon. Strain the sauce and season to taste with salt and pepper. Stir in the lemon juice. Reserve in a warm place.

TO MAKE THE VEGETABLE GARNISH

Heat the butter, thyme and water in a sauté pan. Drop in the shiitake, baby corn, carrots and broccoli, and cook over moderate heat until warmed through. Season to taste with salt and pepper. Reserve and keep warm.

MISE EN PLACE

Vegetable Side (recipe follows)

Spring Rolls (recipe follows)

Mirin Sauce (recipe follows)

4, 12 ounce veal chops
(also called bone-in ribeye of veal)

1 tablespoon vegetable oil

Salt and freshly ground black pepper

FOR THE VEGETABLE SIDE

4 shiitake mushrooms – stem removed

8 baby corn, preferably fresh, cooked

4 asparagus spears cut on a bias, cooked

4 baby carrots, peeled and cut on a bias

4 small florets of broccoli, cooked

1 tablespoon butter

1 sprig of thyme

1/4 cup water

Salt and freshly ground black pepper

FOR THE SPRING ROLLS

2 tablespoons vegetable oil (divided use)

8 Thai spring roll wrappers

2 generous tablespoons julienne of carrots

2 generous tablespoons sliced shittakes

1/4 cup julienne of green cabbage

2 generous tablespoons cooked angel-hair pasta

1 egg, whisked with a fork

1 quart peanut oil

TO COOK THE VEAL CHOP

Preheat a large sauté pan. Season both sides of the veal with salt and pepper. Add the oil to the pan. When the oil begins to smoke, add the veal chops. Sauté the veal for 5-6 minutes on each side for medium rare. Remove from the pan and allow the meat to rest for 10-12 minutes before serving. Unless you have a big enough pan, this step will probably have to be done twice to accommodate all 4 chops.

TO FRY THE SPRING ROLLS

Preheat a fryer or a pot filled halfway with vegetable oil and heat to 350°. Fry the rolls until golden brown and they begin to float. Remove rolls and place on a clean towel or paper towels to drain.

ASSEMBLY

Ladle 1-1/2 ounces of the mirin sauce on the middle of each of the 4 plates. Place 2 spring rolls in the middle of the sauce. Lean the veal on top of the 2 rolls. Carefully place some of the vegetables on top of the veal and serve.

FOR THE MIRIN SAUCE

1 teaspoon vegetable oil

1 cup demi-glace

1 stalk lemon grass, tough outer leaves removed to white part

1 shallot, chopped

1 clove garlic chopped

1/2 cup mirin

2 tablespoons rice wine vinegar

1/2 teaspoon fresh lime juice

PARSLIED RACK OF LAMB *with Chickpea Salad*

Again, I can not recommend strongly enough that you use domestic (Colorado) lamb only. The chickpea salad is my version of a tabbouleh salad substituting chickpeas for bulger wheat.

TO MAKE LAMB SAUCE

Have the butcher save the bone and fat trimmings from the rack of lamb. Roast the lamb scraps in a pan until brown. Drain the fat and add 1/2 cup mire poi and 2 smashed cloves of garlic. Deglaze pan with 1/2 cup of white wine. Add 1 cup of veal stock and reduce until the sauce coats the back of a spoon. Add a 1 1/2 tablespoons of Burleson clover honey and simmer. Add a sprig of fresh thyme and pass through a fine strainer. Season with salt and pepper.

TO MAKE THE CHICK-PEA SALAD

Cover the ckickpeas with water in a large pot over moderate heat and cook about 1 1/2 to 2 hours. Strain the cooked peas and run under cold water. Add the remaining ingredients to the cooled chickpeas. Season with salt and pepper.

TO COOK THE RACK OF LAMB

Season the rack of lamb with salt and pepper. Place the lamb in a non-stick sauté pan and lightly brown on both sides. Place in a 425° oven for 20 minutes for medium-rare temperature. Remove the lamb from pan and let rest on a separate plate for 10 minutes.

ASSEMBLY

Brush the rack of lamb with the dijon mustard. Pat the chopped parsley on top of the rack of lamb. Place the chick pea salad in the middle of four plates. Slice the lamb into 8 chops and place around the chick pea salsa. Drizzle the honey lamb sauce around the lamb chops.

MISE EN PLACE

Lamb Sauce (recipe follows)

Chick-pea Salad (recipe follows)

Cooking instructions for Rack of Lamb

FOR THE LAMB SAUCE

Bone and trimmings from rack of lamb

1/2 cup mire poi

2 smashed cloves of garlic

1/2 cup of white wine

1 cup of veal stock

1 1/2 cup of Burleson clover honey

1 sprig of fresh thyme

salt and pepper

FOR THE CHICKPEA SALAD

1 cup dried chickpeas

2 tablespoons chopped mint

1 tablespoon chopped flat parsley

2 cloves roasted garlic – chopped fine

2 tablespoons finely sliced scallions

2 tablespoons lime juice

3 tablespoons olive oil

4 ounces of feta cheese

FOR THE RACK OF LAMB

1 rack of domestic lamb – frenched

salt and pepper

1/2 cup chopped flat parsley

1 tablespoon dijon mustard

If you do not want to make 'traditional' steak tartar, my version is 'lighter' — no ketchup, mustard or brandy. The addition of the white truffle oil adds a new dimension to the entire dish. Plus, the presentation is stunning. In fact, a meal of tartar, french fries and a nice salad sounds good to me right now.

ASSEMBLY

In a non-reactive bowl, mix together the sirloin, shallots, chives, capers and extra virgin olive oil. Season with salt and pepper. Reserve, keeping cool. Place a long strip of cucumber on the inside of the ring. This will hold the tartar in place when the ring is removed. Put the sirloin tartar in the middle of the "cucumber ring". Lightly pat down into place. Mix the greens with vinaigrette and fried shallot rings and place 1/4 of the mixture atop the tartar. Remove the ring and drizzle each plate with 1 tablespoon of white truffle oil and cracked pepper.

INGREDIENTS

1 pound prime sirloin or tenderloin, cut into 1/8" dice

1 medium shallot, finely diced

3 tablespoons nonpareil capers, 1/2 chopped and 1/2 left whole

4 English cucumber strips, cut thinly lengthwise with a mandoline

4 tablespoons white truffle oil

6 tablespoons extra virgin olive oil

1 cup mixed greens such as frisée, mizuna and baby red oak lettuces

1 tablespoon vinaigrette

4 tablespoons sliced shallots, fried

1 tablespoon finely chopped chives

salt and pepper

SPECIAL EQUIPMENT

4 ring molds: 2 1/2" diameter x 1 1/4" high stainless steel rings

FOIE GRAS
CAVIAR
KOBE BEEF

N PARIS

INDULGE YOURSELF

"There are a few things that even I realize are over-the-top, too expensive, and truly indulgent, but nonetheless must be tried at least once in your life."

In some ways, all of my cooking could be termed 'indulgent.' I'm not interested in 'light' recipes, low-calorie dressings or even 'healthy' food if it means that flavor is sacrificed. However, there are a few things that even I realize are over-the-top, too expensive, and truly too indulgent, but should be tried at least once in your life.

Caviar is still at the top of that list. In my opinion – and in a perfect world – it should be served at 31° and eaten right out of the can (with a mother of pearl spoon so that there's no metallic reaction). What can't be avoided is the controversy that surrounds harvesting caviar. Over-fishing the Caspian Sea may lead to the extinction of one or all three types of caviar-producing sturgeon. Your best bet to help preserve the fish is to purchase caviar through a reputable buyer (we use Petrossian) and hope that the Russian economic conditions improve enough to save these special fish for future generations.

Meanwhile, after I've finished the can of caviar, please put the foie gras down in front of me. Just so you know, foie gras in this country is duck liver, not goose liver. (You can only get goose foie gras in Europe.) The most amazing thing about foie gras is that its flavor changes with each cooking method. You can sear it, roast it, bake it, grill it and it comes out...different. A slightly different taste. A slightly different texture. All wonderful. It may be the most versatile food in the world. It goes with virtually any dish and adds another dimension of taste. I confess I order it whenever I see it on a restaurant's menu.

Finally, while I have touched upon the magic qualities of Kobe beef in other sections, I would like to expound upon my obsession. There is no other beef that is comparable. The price alone should convince you that it isn't just a little better than prime beef, it's in another category. If Kobe were sold in a grocery store, you would have to pay over $150 per pound. Today, the finest Wagyu cattle in the world are raised in Texas (which is a story in of itself). While it's a myth that the cattle are fed beer and given daily massages, after eating Kobe you may start to believe it.

While in my opinion, caviar goes with almost anything, it especially goes well with potato. So instead of toast points or blinis, here is another way to enjoy caviar.

TO CUT THE WAFFLE POTATO

Place the mandoline in the ribbed cutter position. Adjust the height to 1/8 inch. Hold the potato in your hand and push down against the ribbed cutter and make one "ruffle" cut potato. While still holding the potato in your hand turn the potato 60-90 degrees and push down on the ribbed cutter again. This should make a waffle cut on the potato. If the potato is too thin or too thick, adjust the setting. Finish cutting the remaining four potatoes. Place the waffle cut potatoes in warm water to remove some of the starch.

TO FRY THE POTATOES

Place the quart of canola oil in a heavy gauge pot. Heat the oil to 340-350 degrees. Remove the potatoes from the water. Pat the potatoes dry. Carefully place 4-5 potatoes in the oil a few at a time. Fry for 1 - 2 minutes until golden brown and crispy. Remove the cooked chips from the oil and drain on a paper towel. Sprinkle with salt.

ASSEMBLY

Place a large Quenelle or a large teaspoonful of caviar on the plate at a 6 o'clock position. Place a dollop of sour cream at a 9 o'clock position and 1/2 tsp. fresh chives in the middle of the plate. Alternatively place 4-6 waffle potatoes at the 12 o'clock position. Garnish with fresh bouquet of herbs or fresh flowers. Enjoy.

INGREDIENTS

8 ounces Sevruga or Osetra Caviar

4 large Idaho Potatoes to make 24 waffle potato slices

6 ounces sour cream

1 tablespoon finely diced chives

1 quart canola oil

CINNAMON SMOKED SAUTÉED FOIE GRAS
over Sweet Corn Polenta

The flavors of this dish sound daunting, but the cinnamon and foie gras marry fantastically. The sweet corn polenta adds a fresh southwestern element.

TO MAKE FOIE GRAS

Devein and clean foie gras, cut into 8 equal slices, about 2 ounces each. Puree the 2 end slices and reserve. Dust remaining 6 slices with cinnamon and salt. Cold smoke foie gras slices over cinnamon stick and maple wood for 15 minutes (see below). Sear foie gras slices in a dry skillet over medium heat until golden on both sides.

TO PREPARE POLENTA

Bring milk and cream, 1 teaspoon butter, thyme and garlic to a simmer for 20 minutes. Stir mixture as needed. Add corn, simmer 2 more minutes. Remove from heat, stir in foie gras puree. Season this mixture with salt and pepper, reserve and keep warm.

Sauté asparagus tips rapidly in 2 teaspoons of butter, reserve and keep warm.

ASSEMBLY

Spoon polenta into warm soup bowl, top with a slice of foie gras. Garnish with asparagus spears and a ribbon of demi-glaze.

Cold smoking: place foie gras slices on small roasting rack that will fit inside the roasting pan you will use for the wood chips. Place chips in small roasting pan over medium heat, covering pan with aluminum foil. When chips start to smoke, quickly lift foil and place Foie Gras rack over the chips and recover. Remove from direct heat. Smoke for 5 minutes, remove and cool.

Note: Recipe can be scaled up with the same proportions.

INGREDIENTS

1 grade A (or grade B) Foie Gras

1 1/4 teaspoon cinnamon

1 teaspoon salt

1 cinnamon stick

1/2 cup green maple wood chips

1 cup whole milk + 1/2 cup heavy cream

3 tablespoons unsalted butter

1 tablespoon fresh thyme, chopped

1/4 teaspoon fresh garlic, minced

1/3 cup white cornmeal

3 ears sweet corn, freshly shucked

24 pencil asparagus spears, blanched

1 cup demi – glace

BELUGA CAVIAR
with Potato Blini Stack, Crème Fraiche and Clarified Butter

When I was a child traveling with my parents in San Francisco, my father ordered a dish very similar to this. It was the most amazing and dramatic dish I had ever seen (I was afraid to try it.) The memory of that evening – and his enjoyment of the caviar – has remained with me to this day. Was that the starting point for my career path? Perhaps, for I have spent countless enjoyable hours perfecting my version of the dish my father ordered over 25 years ago.

TO MAKE THE BLINI

Cook the potatoes in a pot of salted water, cooking for about 20 minutes or until just done. Put the cooked potatoes through a ricer and reserve. Add the flour and baking powder and mix well with a whip. Slowly add the milk and butter. Incorporate the eggs and season with salt and pepper. The batter should resemble pancake batter. Strain through a fine strainer. Heat a well-seasoned or non-stick pan until warm over medium heat. Carefully ladle into the pan silver dollar sized blinis. Cook on one side and then flip over to brown the other side. Repeat this process until you have used all the batter. Reserve in a warm place.

TO CLARIFY THE BUTTER

Gently warm the butter. As it warms, foam will accumulate on the surface. With a thin metal spoon, skim foam away. Carefully pour off the clarified butter into another pot, leaving behind the milky butter solids on the bottom.

ASSEMBLY

Place a potato blini in the center of each serving plate. Spoon 2 tablespoons of the crème fraiche on the blini. Place a teaspoon of the caviar on top the crème fraiche. Top with another blini and repeat the process until all is used. This will resemble a stack of pancakes topped with crème fraiche and caviar. Drizzle 2 tablespoons of the butter around the stack. Scatter the chives and red onions around each plate. Serve immediately.

MISE EN PLACE

Potato Blini (recipe follows)

4 ounces beluga caviar – osetra or sevruga may be substituted

1/2 cup clarified butter

1/2 cup crème fraiche

1/4 small red onion, finely minced

1 teaspoon finely minced chives

FOR THE BLINI

4 Yukon Gold potatoes, peeled and cut in half

1/2 cup all-purpose flour

2 teaspoons baking powder

1 cup milk, room temperature

4 ounces unsalted butter, melted

2 eggs, room temperature and lightly beaten

salt and pepper

You can't get any more classic than this. Fresh, whole lobes of foie gras are marinated and baked in a very slow oven, which separates the majority of the fat. (Using sel rose prevents the oxidization of the liver, keeping that healthy pink color.) A 24 ounce terrine will hold exactly 2 lobes, enough for a party of 6-8. Keeps two weeks.

TO MAKE THE TERRINE

Remove the lobes of foie gras from the packaging and place in a large bowl. Let the foie gras rest at room temperature for 1 hour. (They'll be easier to handle.) Being careful not to break up the lobes too much, try to remove as many of the large veins as possible with your fingers and the tip of a paring knife. If the lobes do break up, it's all right but it's better to have the pieces as large as possible to go into the terrine, so you won't get a mutilated look. Mix the sel rose with the sauterne and Madeira. Pour over the lobes of foie gras and gently rub in the salt and pepper. Cover the bowl tightly with plastic wrap and let marinate for 6-8 hours. Discard the marinade.

Preheat oven to 250°. Line the terrine mold with plastic wrap, leaving extra plastic hanging off all sides. Carefully pour off the marinade. Place the lobes of foie gras in the terrine and press down as tightly as possible to eliminate any air pockets. Bring the edges of the plastic wrap over the top of the terrine. Don't worry, the plastic wrap won't melt.

Prepare a water bath by using a roasting pan that will accommodate the terrine mold. Place the terrine in the pan and fill the pan with hot water, coming up about 1/3 to 1/2 way up the sides of the terrine. Bake for 30-40 minutes. Remove the terrine from the oven and let rest for 1 hour. Remove the terrine from the water bath and peel back the plastic. With the edge of a spoon or spatula, scrape and discard as much of the fat as possible that has accumulated on the top of the terrine. Save the fat for use later. Recover loosely with plastic and refrigerate for 1 hour.

While cooling, cut a piece of heavy cardboard to fit snugly inside the top of the terrine and wrap a brick with foil. When foie gras has been in the refrigerator for 1 hour, spoon off any additional oil, place the cardboard on the terrine and then the brick. This compression will allow the foie gras to settle tightly in the mold. Refrigerate for at least 24 hours or up to one week.

FOR THE SPAETZLE

Break 6 eggs into a bowl. Whisk in the flour until evenly incorporated. Taste and season with salt and pepper. The batter should resemble very thick pancake batter.

MISE EN PLACE

Foie Gras Terrine

Celery Root and Spaetzle Salad

FOR THE TERRINE

2 "A" grade lobes of foie gras

2 teaspoons sel rose (see sources)

2 tablespoons sauterne or brandy

2 tablespoons Madeira – medium sweet

1/2 teaspoon freshly ground white pepper

1/2 teaspoon salt

SPECIAL EQUIPMENT

1 24 ounce earthenware terrine mold, such as Le Creuset

Spaetzle extruder

FOR THE SPAETZLE

6 eggs

2 cups all-purpose flour

salt and pepper

FOR THE CELERY ROOT SALAD

1 celery root, about 4-inches in diameter, peeled and cut into a fine julienne

1/2 Granny Smith apple, cut into a julienne

2 tablespoons tomato concassé, cut into a julienne

1 teaspoon minced chives

2 tablespoons whole grain mustard

2 tablespoons extra virgin olive oil

1 teaspoon champagne vinegar

salt and pepper

Fill a 4-quart pot with salted water. Pour some of the batter in the hopper of the spaetzle extruder and slide back and forth. Cook for 2 minutes and remove with a slotted scooper into a bowl of ice water. Repeat each batch until the hopper is empty. Drain and refrigerate.

FOR THE SALAD
Toss the celery root, apple, tomato, chives, mustard, olive oil, vinegar and the spaetzle together. Mix thoroughly. Season the salad with salt and pepper and reserve.

ASSEMBLY
Remove the terrine from the mold by rapping a corner lightly against the counter. Carefully remove the plastic wrap and slice the foie gras into four 3/4" slices. Wrap up the rest of the terrine with fresh plastic and refrigerate.

Divide the salad between the plates, placing it in the center. Carefully top the salads with a slice of terrine and garnish with micro-greens or flat leaf Italian parsley. Serve.

FOIE GRAS IN MILK
FOR TERRINE

GRILLED FOIE GRAS
on a Rhubarb Tart with White Pepper Fruit Glaze

I'm amazed that grilling is not used more often as a way to prepare foie gras. I love what grilling adds — new dimensions both of taste and texture. The rhubarb is there as both a tart and sweet element while the white pepper adds a hot 'ping' to this dish.

TO MAKE THE RHUBARB TART

For dough, mix the yeast and the warm water. Let sit for 10 minutes. Place the flour in the food processor and with the motor running add the warm yeast mixture. Add the cold water, oil, honey and salt. Mix until the dough begins to gather. Do not over-mix. If the dough is too dry, add a little cold water. Remove from the machine and place in a bowl, covering with a damp cloth. Place in a warm place to rise. After the dough has risen 2 – 3 times in volume, sprinkle a level surface lightly with flour and roll out the dough in a rectangle about 3/4 – 1" in thick. Sprinkle with more flour if the dough begins to stick. Place the butter on the dough leaving a margin of about 1" around the edges. Fold the dough into thirds, sealing the edges. Roll the dough again into roughly the same rectangular shape, 1" thick. Let it rest, covered, for 30 – 45 minutes. Cut the dough into 2 ounce portions.

TO MAKE THE RHUBARB FILLING

Roughly cut 2 of the rhubarb ribs. Heat the 1 tablespoon butter in a sauté pan and sweat the rhubarb. Add the sugar and continue to cook until it becomes thick and bubbly. Remove from the heat and add the vinegar and honey. Chill. Slice the rest of the rhubarb 1/8" thick. Heat 1 tablespoon butter in a pan and sauté the rhubarb just until limp. Remove from the fire and reserve.

TO MAKE THE FRUIT GLAZE

Combine the dried fruits, water and orange juice in a saucepan. Split the vanilla bean and scrape out the seeds. Add the seeds to the saucepan. Cook over high heat until the mixture is thick and syrupy. Add the pepper, remove from the heat and cool. When the mixture is cool, add the mint. Reserve at room temperature.

TO ASSEMBLE THE TART

If you have a pizza stone, this would be a good time to use it. Preheat the oven at 425° for 1 hour. If you don't have a pizza stone, you can place the tart on a heavy duty baking sheet or two regular baking sheets stacked on each other. Roll out the 2-ounce balls of dough to 4" circles. Brush the rolled dough with extra virgin olive oil and sprinkle with a little salt. Spread some of the rhubarb pulp mixture on the tart shell, leaving a slight edge. Then evenly layer the rhubarb on top of the pulp. Place in

MISE EN PLACE

Rhubarb Tart (recipe follows)

1 lobe Grade "A" foie gras

6 ounces white pepper Fruit Glaze (recipe follows)

FOR THE RHUBARB TART

6 ounces Pizza Pastry Dough (recipe follows)

4 ribs of rhubarb

2 tablespoons butter (divided use)

1/2 cup granulated sugar

1 teaspoon balsamic vinegar

1 teaspoon honey

FOR THE PIZZA PASTRY DOUGH

3 cups flour

1/8 cup warm water

1 package active dry yeast

2/3 cup cold water

1 tablespoon extra virgin olive oil

2 teaspoons honey

1 teaspoon salt

4 ounces butter, cut into small squares and softened

extra virgin olive oil for brushing

kosher salt

FOR THE WHITE PEPPER FRUIT GLAZE

2 tablespoons dried cherries

2 tablespoons dried blueberries

2 tablespoons dried cranberries

2 cups water

1/4 cup orange juice

1/4 vanilla bean

1 teaspoon finely chopped mint

1 teaspoon fresh cracked white pepper

the oven for 5-6 minutes or until the dough is browned and crisp on the bottom. If you aren't using a pizza stone it may take an additional 5 minutes.

ASSEMBLY

To make the foie gras: Slice the foie gras into 4 equal pieces, season with salt and pepper and sauté for 15 – 20 seconds on each side. Place a tart in the center of each serving dish. Place a slice of foie gras on top of the tart and spoon a dollop of the white pepper fruit glaze on the foie gras and serve immediately.

ROASTED FOIE GRAS

Serves 6-8

To me, this is the most luxurious (and unfortunately the most expensive way) to eat foie gras. Many restaurants cannot accommodate this technique because it is meant to serve 6 - 8 people. When the lobe is roasted and sliced, it eats quite differently than a slice of foie gras that has been prepared for an individual serving. This is pure nirvana.

Preheat oven to 400°. Generously season the lobe of foie gras. Heat a sauté pan until moderately hot. Place the foie gras in the pan flat side down and sear for 1 – 2 minutes. Turn over and repeat the process. Place the herbs in the pan with the foie gras and place in the oven. Every few minutes, baste the lobe with the fat that has been rendered. Cook for 20 minutes and remove from the pan. Place the lobe on a plate to bleed for 1 – 2 minutes. Do not discard the fat. When ready to serve, slice the foie gras into 1/2 – 3/4" slices and serve immediately. The foie gras should be crisp on the outside and a succulent, velvety consistency on the inside.

INGREDIENTS

1 large lobe of Grade "A" foie gras

2 fresh bay leaves

1 large sprig of thyme

Salt & pepper

To my way of thinking, this is the best of all possible worlds. Here, kobe beef has replaced tuna in a classic sushi dish and is topped with seared foie gras.

FOR THE KOBE BEEF

Season the kobe beef with salt and pepper. Place the beef over an open flame and lightly sear the outside. Then immediately place the kobe beef into an ice bath to stop the cooking process. Remove the kobe beef from the water and pat dry. Wrap the dry kobe beef in a paper towel and refrigerate until ready to use.

FOR THE DAIKON SALAD

Run the julienned daikon, carrot under cold water for 20 minutes, pat dry. Then add the julienned shiso leaf, olive oil and lime juice to the julienned carrot and daikon. Toss well. Reserve in the refrigerate until ready to use.

TO PLATE

Slice the kobe beef into even slices; place them in a strip on a plate, slightly overlapping the slices. Preheat a non-stick sauté pan over very high heat. Season each slice of foie gras with salt and pepper. Place the seasoned foie gras in the pan and sauté for 15 seconds on each side. Remove the foie gras from the pan and allow to drain on a towel for a few seconds. Place a seared foie gras slice on top of the sliced kobe beef. The place equal amounts of daikon and carrot salad on the top of each seared foie gras. Drizzle the plate with ponzu sauce and serve.

MISE EN PLACE

4 ounces Kobe beef, cut into a slab 3" long by 1" thick

2-1/2" thick slice of Fresh Foie Gras

2 tablespoons Ponzu Sauce (see page 87)

3 tablespoon Daikon Salad

2 edible pansies

FOR THE DAIKON SALAD

1 medium carrot, peeled and julienned

1 daikon root, peeled and julienned

1 Shiso leaf, julienned

1 tablespoon olive oil

1 teaspoon lime juice

ADDING CONTRAST TO THE PLATE

"The truth is, we don't appreciate vegetables as part of fine dining in this country."

In the culinary world, there has been a lot of attention paid in the last 10 years to 'seasonality' – and for good reason. It makes sense to use vegetables when they are at the peak of their flavor. But because of greenhouse production, it is now possible to procure almost any vegetable I want at almost any time of year, with a few notable exceptions. Two of those exceptions are heirloom tomatoes and mushrooms (heirloom tomatoes, with their one-of-kind flavor are literally the genetic source of all other tomatoes, and are in season only in the summer; and yes, Morels, Chanterelles and Porcini mushrooms all have their growing seasons, too).

An even bigger issue for me, however, is variety. It's not that I don't have enough variety among vegetables to choose from, but that my customers are unwilling to accept a real variety. This is one area where I feel Americans are being provincial and missing out in the bargain. For example, while I have been able to slowly introduce ramps (baby leeks), salsify (a white root), trevisse (purple lettuce), fava beans and a few other non-standard vegetables, on the whole, it's definitely been an uphill battle. The truth is, we don't appreciate vegetables as part of fine dining in this country. We do, however, love our starches (I'm guilty, too). My current three starch favorites are mousseline potatoes (extremely fine mashed potatoes flavored with celery root, garlic or horseradish), polenta, and risotto. Risotto remains a classic partly because it is so difficult to cook correctly. No other dish requires as much of my attention, and is so worth the effort. I advise you to flavor your risotto as you will with this proviso: if you add cheese to it, never serve it with fish.

Side dishes may never have the spotlight on them, but with a little attention and imagination, sometimes they are what we remember about a meal.

ARTICHOKE CAKES

Like any fried cake (crab, potato, etc.) but with artichokes. Watch out for the Tabasco, this recipe needs a little, but not too much.

Combine the artichoke, potato, egg, thyme, chives, lime juice, 1 teaspoon Worcestershire sauce and Tabasco in non-reactive bowl. Use fork to mix. Season to taste, form into 4 small circular cakes. Heat oil in heavy skillet over medium heat. Sauté cakes until golden brown. Turn, cook second side and serve immediately.

Note: Recipe can be scaled up in direct proportions.

INGREDIENTS

1 pound fresh artichoke bottoms simmered and finely diced

1 medium baked potato peeled and shredded

1 whole egg, lightly beaten

1 clove garlic, minced

1 tablespoon fresh thyme, chopped

1 tablespoon fresh chives, chopped

1 tablespoon fresh lime juice

1 tsp Worcestershire sauce

2 drops Tabasco sauce

salt

black pepper, freshly ground

3 tablespoons canola oil

CARAMELIZED RED ONION MARMALADE

This is a way of cooking red onions into a syrup (it will be maroon in colorization). To be used with the Pan Seared Scallops.

In a large, heavy non-reactive saucepan combine the onions and brown sugar and cook over moderate heat, stirring often until the onions begin to caramelize and turn golden 20-25 minutes. Stir in the wine and vinegar. Increase the heat to a moderately high and bring to a boil. Reduce the heat to moderately low and cook, stirring often until most of the liquid has evaporated – about 15 minutes. Season to taste with salt and pepper and set aside to cool. Serve at room temperature

The onion marmalade can be made up to three weeks ahead.

INGREDIENTS

2 large red onions thinly sliced

3 tablespoons of brown sugar

3/4 cups dry red wine

3 tablespoons balsamic vinegar

salt and freshly ground pepper

FRESH PASTA *with Arugula, Tomatoes and Shaved Parmesan* *Serves 4-6*

Very light and easy to prepare. (Making your own pasta at home has gone in and out of vogue, but there really is no substitute. Just look at the difference in cooking times below.)

TO MAKE

In large pot bring 5 quarts of water to a rolling boil over high heat. Meanwhile using a vegetable peeler, shave the parmesan cheese into long thick strips into a large warmed serving bowl using a vegetable peeler. Add the arugula, tomatoes and olive oil, tossing to blend.

Stir sea salt and pasta into the boiling water and cook until tender but firm, 2-3 minutes for dried pasta, 15 seconds for fresh pasta. Stir to prevent sticking. Drain the pasta in a colander, add to the arugula mixture and toss. Season to taste with sea salt and plenty of freshly ground pepper. Divide the pasta into warm serving bowls and serve immediately.

INGREDIENTS

2 ounce chunk of Parmigiano-Reggiano cheese

4 cups arugula leaves, stemmed, rinsed, and dried

4 ripe plum tomatoes, about 1/2 pound , coarsely chopped

1/4 cup extra virgin olive oil

3 tablespoons sea salt

1 pound fresh pasta, such as (preferably papardelle)

freshly ground pepper

GRATIN OF TOMATOES AND GRILLED PEPPERS
with Roasted Polenta

Polenta is the star of this recipe. I love how versatile it is. You can eat it soft and hot or let it cool, cut it into squares and grill it for another taste and texture. (Feel free to use instant polenta. It actually works very well.)

Oil an 8" pie pan. In a medium saucepan bring two cups of water to a boil, whisk in the polenta. Reduce the heat to a very low and cook, 4-5 minutes until the polenta pulls away from the pan. Season with sea salt and black pepper to taste and stir in the butter. Pour into the prepared pan and let cool.

Roast peppers directly over a gas flame or under the broiler as close to the heat as possible, turning until charred all over. Transfer the peppers to a paper or plastic bag close tightly and let steam for 5 minutes. Using a small sharp knife scrape the blackened skin and halve them lengthwise. Remove the cores, seeds, and membranes and discard. Slice the peppers in 1/2" strips.

Preheat the oven to 400°. Use a little of the olive oil to coat the bottom of a 9" gratin dish. Arrange a layer of the peppers in the bottom of the dish. Sprinkle with a little garlic, the anchovies, tomatoes, crushed red pepper, and some sea salt. Moisten with a few drops of olive oil. Continue layering the ingredients in this way ending with a layer of peppers. Drizzle the remaining olive oil on top and bake for 20 minutes. Remove from the oven and cover tightly to keep warm.

Preheat the broiler. Unmold polenta and cut into 4 wedges. Arrange the polenta on a lightly oiled baking sheet and broil for 5 minutes. Do this on each side or until browned at the edges.

ASSEMBLY

Place the polenta on 4 plates. Arrange the peppers and tomatoes in a small mound alongside and drizzle a spoonful of the juices. Garnish with basil leaves.

MISE EN PLACE

1/2 cup instant polenta

sea salt

freshly ground black pepper

1 tablespoon unsalted butter

2 medium red bell peppers

2 medium yellow bell peppers

3-4 tablespoons extra virgin oil

2 small garlic cloves, sliced paper thin

4 anchovy fillets, cut in the small pieces

1/2 teaspoon crushed red pepper

6 large plum tomatoes, peeled, seeded and cut in small chunks

1/4 cup coarsely chopped flat leaf parsley

12 small green or purple basil leaves

GRANDMA'S SPAGHETTI GRAVY

This is the real deal. My great great grandmother's spaghetti 'gravy' so called because it can go over any pasta including lasagna. Passed down for generations (my mother's maiden name was Cereghino) this is the first time it's been out of the family. Enjoy.

Brown round steak, cut into small strips. Soak porcini mushrooms in 1 cup of very warm water for 30 minutes. Remove the mushrooms, squeezing out excess juice. Reserve the mushroom juice. Into a very large pot, pour the four cans of tomato sauce and water, salt and pepper to taste. Add 2 cloves of garlic and 1 bay leaf. Simmer on the back of the stove. Add the remaining mushroom juice. Grind together in a blender or cuisinart the steak, parsley, onion, celery leaves, mushrooms and bell peppers, until mixture has a fine texture.

Heat 3-4 tablespoons of olive oil in a large sauté pan. Add the mixture from the blender. Occasionally add some of the tomato sauce mixture to keep the contents moist. Simmer for about half a hour until brown.

Transfer all the browned ingredients to the tomato sauce, and simmer slowly for 4-5 hours.

This sauce freezes well for later use.

INGREDIENTS

1 pound top round steak

1 large handful fresh parsley

1 large onion

1 large handful celery leaves

1 large green bell pepper

.5 ounce package porcini dried mushrooms

4 cans of tomato sauce, 8 ounces each

32 ounces of water

OVERLY BUTTERED POTATOES (MOUSSELINE)

The ingredient list should include elbow grease. These take a little effort (to pass them through the chinois) but once you taste them, you will never want regular mashers again.

Submerge the 2 quartered potatoes in a pot covered with water. Add 1-tablespoon salt to the water; cook the potatoes until just done, about 30 minutes. Strain the potatoes and pass through a ricer. Return the riced potatoes to the pot and add the butter and the cream, stirring until incorporated. Season with salt and pepper. To make the potatoes even smoother, pass them through a chinois. This is an arduous task but is well worth the smooth, silky result.

INGREDIENTS

2 large idaho potatoes, peeled & cut into quarters

1 pound unsalted butter

1 cup heavy cream

salt and pepper

GRILLED ASPARAGUS *and Caper Bacon Dressing*

History has not recorded who first thought of grilling asparagus, but it was a good idea. This vinaigrette is one of my favorites.

TO PREPARE THE ASPARAGUS

Preheat a grill. Lightly brush the peeled and blanched asparagus with oil, season with salt and pepper. Place on the grill for 1-2 minute remove and keep warm.

TO MAKE CAPER/BACON VINAIGRETTE

Place the rendered bacon in a sauté pan heat of the extra virgin olive oil. Sauté bacon for 1 minute, add the capers, and cook till they begin to open up like a flower pod. Remove from the heat; add the tomato concassé, extra virgin olive oil and the balsamic vinegar. Incorporate the chiffonade romaine lettuce. Season with salt and pepper, add the soy sauce.

ASSEMBLY

Place 6 asparagus on each plate. Spoon the caper/bacon vinaigrette on top of the asparagus. Place the batonnaise chives and chiffonade basil on top of the caper vinaigrette.

INGREDIENTS

24 jumbo asparagus peeled and blanched

1/2 cup cooked slab bacon, cut in 1/2" dice

1/8 cup diced tomato concassé

1 tablespoon nonpareil capers

1/2cup chiffonade romaine lettuce

1/8 cup batonnaise chives

1/3 cup extra virgin olive oil

2 tablespoons balsamic vinegar

1 tablespoon lite soy sauce

3 leaves basil chiffonade

POTATO CHIPS

Make sure you soak the sliced potatoes in warm water first to remove some of the starch. Experiment with different seasonings.

Slice the potatoes on a mandoline paper-thin. Soak the sliced potatoes in cold water for 1 – 2 hours. This will remove the excess starch and keep the potatoes from discoloring.

Blend the spices together thoroughly.

Preheat 2 quarts of frying oil to 350°. While the oil is heating, remove the potatoes from the water and drain. Thoroughly pat them dry with paper towels to remove the excess water. If the potatoes are not dry, they will spatter when put in the oil. Fry the potatoes in batches, turning them occasionally. When golden brown, remove them from the oil with a slotted spoon and dry on paper towels or brown paper sacks. Sprinkle with the seasoning salt and serve.

MISE EN PLACE

2 russet potatoes, peeled

Seasoning Salt (recipe follows)

SEASONING SALT

1 ounce kosher salt

1 tablespoon ounce finely ground black pepper

2 teaspoons ground cumin

2 teaspoons garlic powder

1 teaspoon onion powder

ROOT VEGETABLE AU GRATIN

Serves 4

Similar to potatoes au gratin, but adding beets, carrots, parsnips and celery root. This may be a way to get picky eaters to eat their vegetables.

Preheat oven to 325°. Prepare an 8"x8" brownie pan by rubbing with butter. Using a mandoline slice the potatoes, parsnip, carrot & potato to 1/6" thickness. Rub the chopped garlic on the bottom of the buttered 8"x8" pan. Then randomly layer the root vegetables over the garlic. Mix the 2 eggs and the quart of cream in a bowl. Season with salt and pepper. Pour the egg-cream mixture over sliced root vegetables. Sprinkle the Parmigiano-Reggiano over the cream. Place the 8"x8" pan in a larger receptacle. Pour water halfway up the side of the pan and place in a 325° oven. After cooking for 45 minutes, the top of the vegetables will begin to turn brown. Remove the pan from the oven and cover with aluminum foil. Return the pan to the oven and cook for an additional 1 1/2-2 hours or until the root vegetable gratin is soft when pierced by a knife. Remove from the oven and let rest for 20 minutes before serving.

To serve, cut the gratin with a sharp paring knife. Remove carefully with a thin, flexible spatula.

INGREDIENTS

1 celery root, peeled

2 parsnips peeled

1 large idaho potato, peeled

1 jumbo carrot, peeled

1 quart heavy cream

2 eggs, beaten

2 cloves of garlic, finely chopped

salt and pepper

1/2 cup grated Parmigiano-Reggiano

SPICY GRILLED TRAVISSE *with Fresh Mozzarella*

Serves 4

Travisse is the Italian version of radicchio and has a long, skinny leaf (somewhat like romaine). It's best characteristic is that it holds up to grilling (but it definitely needs the tart lemon flavor added). The mozzarella adds a contrasting smoothness and finishes it off.

TO MAKE THE GRILLED RADICCHIO

In medium saucepan of boiling salted water, blanch the heads of travisse until wilted, 2-3 minutes. Transfer to a colander with a slotted spoon. Gently press out as much water possible. Drain well on paper towels.

Light a grill or preheat the broiler. Gently open the leaves of each travisse and place a ball of mozzarella in the center. Top with some of the anchovy and season with salt, black pepper and a pinch of crushed red pepper. Sprinkle with parsley and few drops of olive oil. Carefully enclose the cheese in the leaves, secure each bundle with 2 toothpicks.

INGREDIENTS

4 heads of travisse, 4 ounces each

4 miniature mozzarella balls (bocconcini) drained, 1 ounce each

4 small anchovy fillets, optional

salt and fresh ground black pepper

crushed red pepper

2 teaspoons chopped flat leaf parsley

extra virgin olive oil for drizzling

lemon sections for serving

Lightly brush the travisse with olive oil. Grill over moderate heat and broil, turning once for about 6 minutes or until the travisse is golden brown. Remove the toothpicks and garnish with lemon sections.

LEMON RISOTTO

Serves 4

Risotto – according to me – should be runny, creamy, almost soupy. In some ways, this is the least understood 'pasta.' The lemon helps to lighten this filling dish.

Heat the stock in a medium saucepan and keep it simmering over very low heat. In a small bowl toss the mint, sage and lemon zest together. Set aside.

In a large heavy non-reactive saucepan combine 2 tablespoons of the butter with the oil, shallots and a sprinkling of sea salt. Cook over moderate heat stirring until the shallots are soft and translucent but not brown, about 3 minutes. Add the rice and stir until the grains are well coated with oil and semi – translucent, 1-2 minutes.

Stir a cup of the hot stock into the rice and stir constantly until most of the it has been absorbed, 1-2 minutes. Add another cup of the simmering stock and stir until it has been absorbed. Keep the heat at moderate to maintain a simmer. The rice should always be just barely covered with stock. Repeat this process stirring frequently and tasting regularly until the rice is almost tender but firm, about 17 minutes total. The risotto should have a creamy, porridge- like consistency.

Remove the saucepan from the heat. Stir in the remaining 2 tablespoons of butter, the reserved lemon zest and herbs, lemon juice, 1/2 cup parmesan, sea salt and pepper to taste. Cover and let stand for 2 minutes to allow the flavors to blend. Serve immediately, with additional cheese passed separately.

INGREDIENTS

5 cups chicken stock, preferably homemade

1 teaspoon chopped fresh mint

1 teaspoon chopped fresh sage

1 1/2 teaspoons finely grated lemon zest

4 tablespoons unsalted butter

1 tablespoon extra virgin olive oil

2 shallots minced

sea salt

1 1/2 cups Arborio rice

2 tablespoons fresh grated parmesan cheese plus more for serving

freshly ground pepper

WILD MUSHROOM RISOTTO *with White Truffle Oil*

Only fresh Chanterelles, Morels or Shiitakes (when in season) will do. This has been on the menu since day one at The Mercury. The unique flavor is enhanced with white truffle oil.

FOR THE MUSHROOMS

Heat a large sauté pan over high heat; add the vegetable oil. When oil is smoking, add the mushrooms and sauté for 5-6 minutes, until mushrooms are soft to the touch. Reserve.

FOR THE RISOTTO

Bring the vegetable stock to a simmer and keep warm. Place the two tablespoons of butter in a broad sturdy pan and turn the heat on to medium. When the butter begins to brown, add the onion. Cook and stir until the onion becomes translucent, then add the arborio rice. Stir quickly until all the grains are coated well.

Add 1/2 cup of the hot vegetable stock stirring constantly with a wooden spoon. Continue to stir until all of the liquid is gone. Continue to add the vegetable stock in intervals stirring until liquid is incorporated. Add the sauté mushrooms, the Parmigiano-Reggiano, and the butter. Stir until the risotto looks creamy. Add the white truffle oil, tomato concassé and chives. Season to taste.

TO SERVE

Spoon equal amounts into four bowls and garnish with shaved parmesan cheese.

FOR THE RISOTTO

5 cups vegetable stock

2 cups arborio risotto

2 tablespoons chopped onions

2 tablespoons butter

1/2 cup dry white wine

1/2 cup Parmigiano-Reggiano

2 tablespoons white truffle oil

6 ounces butter

1 tablespoon finely chopped chives

2 tablespoons tomato concassé

FOR THE MUSHROOMS

1/2 cup 1 cup quartered mushrooms

1/2 cup fresh Chanterelles

1 ounce fresh or dried Morels

2 tablespoons vegetable oils

alt and pepper

JALAPEÑO CHEESE GRITS

Southern comfort food with a little kick to it. This can be served at formal dinner parties (it is on my dinner table at Thanksgiving every year and will continue to be) or the most casual affair. I love this dish.

Bring 3 quarts of water to a boil. Add grits and cook according to the directions on the package. Remove the cooked grits from the heat and add the milk, eggs, butter, cheese, jalapeños, Worcestershire, and salt/pepper. Pour into a greased 8"x12" cake pan and cook at 350° for 45 minutes, or until knife inserted into grits comes out clean.

INGREDIENTS

3 quarts water

3 cups grits

9 eggs, beaten

6 cups grated cheddar cheese

3 cups milk

10 ounces butter

1/2 cup seeded and finely minced jalapeños

2 teaspoons Worcestershire sauce

salt and pepper to taste

SWEETS

A RESTAURANT'S LAST CHANCE

"One secret of our

soufflés: we liberally line

the white porcelain

baking molds with both

butter and sugar.

The sugar helps conduct

heat evenly."

Consider this: dessert may be the most important dish a restaurant serves. Because it finishes the meal, it's the last impression the patron takes from the restaurant. That being said, I confess that I have never been a pastry chef. It really is another career path in this profession. (I freely admit one reason it never appealed to me: I didn't enjoy the constant feeling of flour and sugar on my hands.)

I'm not immune, however, to the lure of desserts (as you can see from the length of this chapter). In the restaurants, however, we limit our dessert offerings to seven. Hopefully this ensures that each one will be memorable, leaving each guest with that proverbial good taste in their mouth.

Our best-selling dessert is the souffle. I'm quite sure we don't do anything differently in the way we prepare it, I just like to think we do it extraordinarily well. I love the simplicity of a souffle. Beaten egg whites, pastry cream, sugar and flavoring. Then allowing nature to create this eye appealing indulgence. I don't know why people think that souffles are so difficult to make. They're not. I urge you to try a souffle recipe. Relax.

My favorite 'flavor' is still Grand Marnier but if you think you might want something different, try the coconut or chocolate souffle. One secret of our souffle's success: line the white porcelain baking molds with both butter and sugar. The sugar plays a critical role because it conducts heat in such a way as to help evenly cook the souffle.

As for other desserts, I personally tend to favor fresh fruit tarts and certain ice creams (butter pecan) as well as chocolate brownies (but that doesn't expand to include chocolate cake for some reason). Each sweet tooth is different and I encourage you to find yours in this section. Consider desserts another kind of indulgence you deserve at least once in a while.

APPLE TART TATIN

If you love warm apple pie as much as I do, this may be the quintessential way to enjoy it. In this case, however, it's upside down and caramelized. Perfect with ice cream.

Preheat oven to 400°. Place the sugar and water onto the stove over very high heat. When the sugar and water begin to caramelize, watch closely and cook until mixture begins to turn. Remove the caramel from the stove and pour into the bottom of pie pan. Quickly pick the pan up by the rim and tilt to level the caramel.

Heat the butter in a large heavy gauge sauté pan. When the butter begins to brown, add the apple pieces and sauté until al dente, about 5 minutes. Strain the juices from the pan. Arrange the apple pieces on the top of the caramel. Pack the apples together as closely as you can and place the rolled dough on top of the sautéed apples. Tuck the outer edges into the inside of the pan. Brush the top of the pastry with beaten egg.

Place the pie pan containing the tart on a baking sheet and cook it in the oven for 50 minutes, or until the top is nicely browned. Remove the cooked tart from the oven and run a knife around the rim of the pan to loosen the crust. Invert a large plate over the pan. Flip the pan over and rap it against the counter. If any of the apples stick to the bottom of the pan, remove them and place wherever needed on the tart. Reheat the remaining caramel and pour onto the apples. Eat warm or at room temperature.

INGREDIENTS

1/2 recipe for Puff Pastry (see recipe in this chapter) rolled into 12" disc

8 granny smith apples, peeled cored and cut into 1/8ths

2/3 cup sugar

1/3 cup water

2 tablespoons unsalted butter

1 egg, beaten

1 10" pie pan or 10" cake pan

BRIOCHE DOUGH

With this recipe, you will make the finest bread ever. (It also makes great French toast.) It goes wonderfully with foie gras, caviar – even with your favorite jam or jelly.

Mix the yeast, water and sugar in a bowl. Let rest for 5-8 minutes to bloom. Mix together the flour, butter, eggs and salt in the bowl of an electric mixer set to low speed using the paddle attachment. Slowly add the yeast mixture and continue to mix for 8-10 minutes. The dough should have a sticky, glossy appearance. Remove the dough from the mixer and put it in an oiled bowl. Place the bowl in a warm place, covered with a towel. Allow it to rise until it has doubled in size. When the dough has risen, "break" the dough by pushing down on it with your hands, deflating it. Re-form the dough into a ball, place the ball into another bowl and cover with plastic if you are not going to use it immediately. Place in refrigerator until needed.

INGREDIENTS

1 (1/4 ounce) dry yeast

1/4 cup lukewarm water

2 teaspoons granulated sugar

2 1/2 cups bread flour

8 ounces unsalted butter, melted

4 eggs

3/4 teaspoon salt

1 whole egg – beaten

FLOURLESS CHOCOLATE CAKE

Most chefs have a recipe for this type of cake. Some for reasons related to food allergies or dietary constraints. Personally, I make it because it has intense chocolate flavor while at the same time, it's very light. Just a little powdered sugar on top is all it needs to complete. (Whenever I have an urge for chocolate, I'll sneak a piece of this cake from the pantry.)

Preheat oven to 350°. Butter cake pan and dust with sugar. Melt the chocolate and butter in a clean, dry stainless bowl set over a pan of simmering water. Reserve.

Whip the egg yolks and half of the sugar in a mixing bowl. When the beater leaves a path in the frothy yolks, gently fold in the chocolate mixture.

Whip the egg whites until they hold a peak. Slowly add the remaining sugar and whip until the whites are stiff and glossy. Fold the chocolate mixture into the beaten whites until just blended. Do not overmix.

Pour the batter into the cake pan. Bake for 30 minutes. The outer rim of the cake will have set, while the center will be a little shaky. Cool in the pan and invert onto a plate. Dust with confectioner's' sugar.

INGREDIENTS

19 ounces bittersweet chocolate

6 ounces butter, melted

16 egg yolks

16 egg whites

7 ounces granulated sugar

12" cake pan

GRAND MARNIER SOUFFLÉ

There is a mystique about souffles and I'm not sure why. When whipped egg whites are baked, they will rise (it's a law of nature). It does take 20 minutes to bake but even oven doors may be slammed (souffles are durable). You must, however, liberally coat the porcelain molds with butter and sugar. What follows are three additional flavor choices (Grand Marnier is still my favorite). Enjoy.

Preheat Oven to 350°. Place the pastry cream, egg yolks and Grand Marnier in a bowl and mix well. Place the egg whites in a non-reactive bowl and whip to a soft peak. With the mixer running, slowly add the 4 tablespoons of granulated sugar, mix for 30 more seconds. Gently fold the whipped egg whites into the soufflé base. Pour the soufflé base into each of the ramekins. Bake for 20 minutes. Remove from the oven and dust with powdered sugar. Bring to the table and pour the vanilla sauce into the soufflé.

INGREDIENTS

1 cup Pastry Cream (see recipe in this chapter)

3 egg yolks

8 Eggs

4 tablespoons sugar

3 tablespoons Grand Marnier

6 ounces vanilla sauce (see Crème Anglaise recipe in this chapter)

4 heavily buttered and sugared soufflé ramekins

CHOCOLATE SOUFFLÉ

Follow the same procedures as for the Grand Marnier soufflé except add the cocoa powder to the pastry cream base and substitute chocolate sauce for the vanilla sauce

Melt all ingredients in a double boiler until chocolate is melted and mix well. Keep warm until use.

INGREDIENTS

1 cup Pastry Cream (see recipe in this chapter)

3 egg yolks

8 egg whites

4 tablespoons sugar

3 tablespoons cocoa powder

2 tablespoons dark rum

CHOCOLATE SAUCE

9 ounces semi-sweet chocolate

1 cup milk

1/2 cup heavy cream

1/2 cup granulated sugar

COCONUT SOUFFLÉ

Follow the same procedures as for the Grand Marnier Soufflé except add the coconut flakes and malibu rum to the pastry cream base.
Serve with vanilla sauce flavored with coconut flakes.

INGREDIENTS

1 cup Pastry Cream (see recipe in this chapter)

3 egg yolks

3 tablespoons coconut flakes

2 ounces malibu rum

8 egg whites

4 tablespoons sugar

RASPBERRY SOUFFLE

Follow the same procedures as for the Grand Marnier soufflé except add the raspberry pulp to the pastry cream base. Serve with vanilla sauce or sweet whipped cream flavored with raspberry brandy.

INGREDIENTS

1 cup Pastry Cream (see recipe in this chapter)

3 egg yolks

4 tablespoons raspberry pulp- recipe follows

8 egg whites

4 tablespoons sugar

This is a very light and luxurious cheesecake. It is quite airy. This is a difficult dessert to master, but well worth the effort. Do not refrigerate this cheesecake because it will change its density, hence changing the complexion of the cheesecake.

TO MAKE THE CHEESECAKE

Butter and dust an angel-food cake pan with sugar. If the pan is in 2 pieces, wrap the outside of the bottom with foil that comes about halfway up the pan.

In a stainless steel mixing bowl, beat the cream cheese, cottage cheese, sour cream, butter, salt, flour, lemon juice and vanilla until smooth. Add the whole eggs and egg yolks one at a time into the cream cheese mixture, beating briefly between each addition just until smooth. Place the bowl over, but not in simmering water. Whip until the mixture becomes runny. It should resemble a thick creamy soup. Reserve.

Preheat the oven to 300°. Place the sugar and water in a pan and cook until the temperature reaches 220° on a candy thermometer. Occasionally wipe down the sides of the pan with a damp pastry brush to prevent crystallization. While the sugar is cooking, whip the egg whites until stiff. While whipping, slowly drizzle the sugar syrup into the egg whites just until incorporated. Do not over-whip.

Pour about 1/4 of the egg whites into the cheese mixture and mix in to lighten the batter. Fold in the rest of the egg white mixture. Pour into the prepared pan. Place the pan in a roasting pan and fill with about 2 inches of hot water. Bake for 2 – 2 1/2 hours. Remove from the oven and let the pan cool in the water bath for 1 – 2 hours. At this point, the cake will have dropped in volume by one-third. When the cake is at room temperature, invert onto a cake plate. Leave the cake at room temperature and slice into wedges.

TO MAKE THE COMPOTE

Slit the piece of vanilla bean and scrape the seeds into the sugar. Stir and toss with the fruit. Allow the fruit to macerate for 1-2 hours.

ASSEMBLY

If serving dessert individually, serve at room temperature on the side of the cheesecake. If the presentation is family style, spoon compote on top of the cheesecake and serve.

INGREDIENTS

2 pounds cream cheese

1/2 pound cottage cheese

6 ounces sour cream

4 ounces butter, room temperature

1 teaspoon salt

3 ounces flour

2 tablespoons lemon juice, fresh squeezed

2 tablespoons vanilla

7 whole eggs

8 egg yolks

2 cups sugar

1/2 cup water

8 egg whites

Fruit Compote (recipe follows)

FOR THE COMPOTE

1/4 vanilla bean

1 cup raspberries

1/2 cup blackberries

1/2 cup sliced strawberries

1/2 cup blueberries

4 tablespoons sugar

CHOCOLATE "FALLING DOWN" CAKE
with Tahitian Vanilla Sauce

Serves 4

A wonderfully messy, gooey, runny cake, with intense chocolate flavors.(Try not to eat it with your fingers).

PREPARATION

Melt butter and chocolate in double-boiler.

Whip yolks and sugar until they triple in volume. Add the cooled melted chocolate and butter mixture to the yolk and sugar mixture. Slowly add the flour and the cinnamon. Place in the prepared molds and bake at 400° for 7 minutes. Remove the cakes from the oven and turn onto a plate. Pour vanilla sauce around and serve immediately. The cake should be runny inside.

FOR TAHITIAN VANILLA SAUCE

Whip yolks and sugar until they reach a "whitened" state. Boil milk with vanilla bean. Pour scalded milk slowly into egg yolk mixture. Incorporate and return to the stove and cook until the cream coats the back of a spoon. Do not boil or the eggs will solidify. Strain and chill immediately.

INGREDIENTS

4 , 3" cake molds, buttered and floured, tapped clean and floured and buttered again.

1 cup (2 sticks) butter

1 teaspoon cinnamon

9 ounces bittersweet chocolate

1/2 ounce flour

4 egg yolks

4 ounces sugar

FOR THE VANILLA SAUCE

1 pint whole milk

4 ounces sugar

7 egg yolks

1 vanilla bean (split and seeded)

PECAN PIE

Serves 8

I readily admit that I do love pecans, especially when they are caramelized and crunchy. My only problem with this dish is that when the pie has finished cooking, I invariably end up eating the caramelized pecans before I can serve the pie.

Beat eggs, add sugar and corn syrup, then add salt, vanilla and the melted butter. Place the pecans in the bottom of an unbaked pie crust. Add the filling and bake slowly at 350° for 50 –60 minutes. The nuts will rise to the top and form a crusted layer.

INGREDIENTS

1 cup pecan halves

3 eggs

1/2 cup sugar

1 cup dark corn syrup

1/8 teaspoon salt

1 teaspoon vanilla

1/2 cup butter, melted

1 10" pie pan

CRÈME ANGLAISE – *vanilla sauce*

This is what I call a base sauce. All ice creams are made from this sauce. It's also sauce for souffles. Add caramel, raspberry purée, créme de menthe or your favorite flavor.

Whisk the yolks and 1/2 the sugar in a non-reactive bowl. Place the milk, remaining sugar and vanilla bean in a non-reactive saucepan and bring to a rolling boil. Place a small saucer in the pot to prevent the milk from boiling over. Pour the hot milk into the egg yolk mixture and mix well. Pour this back into the pot and slowly cook over low heat. Cook until the sauce coats the back of a spoon and you can draw your finger through it. Strain and put in a non-reactive storage container. Place a piece of plastic wrap on the surface of the sauce and loosely place the lid on the container. Refrigerate. When chilled, secure the lid.

INGREDIENTS

7 egg yolks

2 cups milk

8 ounces sugar

1/2 vanilla bean

CRÈME PÂTISSIÈRE – *pastry cream*

I find endless uses for this cream in my kitchens (for napoleons, eclairs, creme puffs even fresh fruit tarts). It's nice that something so necessary is also so versatile.

Whisk together the egg yolks and 1/2 of the sugar in a non-reactive bowl. Place the milk, remaining sugar and vanilla bean in a non-reactive saucepan and bring to a simmer. Whisk the milk into the egg mixture and return to the pot. Bring to a boil, stirring constantly. The sauce should be quite thick and somewhat paste-like. Pass through a strainer and put in a storage container. Cover the surface of the cream with a piece of plastic wrap and loosely place the lid on the container. Refrigerate. When the mixture has chilled, secure the lid.

INGREDIENTS

2 cups whole milk

1 cup sugar

8 egg yolks

5 ounces unsalted butter (10 tablespoons)

1/2 vanilla bean

PÂTE SABLIS – *sweet pastry dough*

This is a classic butter cookie dough. It also makes a fabulous dough for fresh fruit tarts.

Place all of the ingredients in a mixing bowl. With the paddle attached, mix until it begins to come together. While mixing, the mixture will resemble sand, hence the term sablis, which in French means sand. Remove the dough from the bowl. Form into a ball and refrigerate covered in plastic wrap for 1 hour. This dough can be made up to a week ahead if stored in this manner. I also use the dough for butter cookies.

INGREDIENTS

1 pound flour

6 ounces granulated sugar

6 ounces unsalted butter

1 whole egg

pinch of slat

PÂTE BRISÉE, *unsweetened pie dough*

Place all of the ingredients in the bowl of an electric mixer. With the paddle attachment, mix until the ingredients begin to come together. It should be the consistency of sandy peas. Press down on the dough with your finger and if it doesn't stay together, add a drop or two of water. With your hands, shape the dough into a ball and wrap in plastic. Refrigerate for at least 4 hours.

If you wrap it well, this dough can be made one week in advance.

INGREDIENTS

1 cup flour

3 ounces unsalted butter, cold

1/2 teaspoon sugar

3 tablespoons cold water

Pinch of salt

PUFF PASTRY

This is one of the greatest creations in the history of the culinary world. The way butter and flour work together (with folding) to produce this layered effect is amazing.

Place the butter onto a floured work surface and using a rolling pin, flatten the butter. Sprinkle 3/4 cup of the flour over the butter. With a scraper, "chop" the flour into the butter. Keep scraping until the flour and butter are well combined. Scrape this mixture onto a piece of waxed paper or plastic wrap. With the scraper, form into a square about 10"x10" and refrigerate for 30 minutes.

Place 1-1/4 cups of the flour and the salt onto the work surface or a large cutting board. Make a well in the center and add the cream and the water. Using your fingers, mix the liquid into the flour a little at a time until thoroughly combined. The dough will have a shiny appearance when it's ready. Do not over work. Roll the dough out into a large square approximately. 16"x16". Place the chilled butter square into the middle of the rolled square with each corner of the butter square touching the center of each long side of the larger square; it will look like a diamond inside a square. Fold each of the corners toward the middle of the square. Seal the seams by pinching with your fingers. This should now look like a large square. Sprinkle with flour and slowly roll the dough 3/8" thick into a large rectangle about 24"x12". Fold the rolled dough about two-thirds onto itself. Then fold the remaining dough onto the top of the other fold, you should have a three-fold rectangle about 6"x12". This is your 1st turn of the puff pastry. Refrigerate for 20-30 minutes on a cookie sheet or cutting board covered with a towel. Remove the dough from the refrigerator, place the short open end facing you, uniformly roll the dough into another 24"x12" rectangle. Fold the dough into a three-fold rectangle and refrigerate, repeat this process four more times. The puff pastry will then have the classic 6 folds. Cover tightly until ready to use. The puff pastry will also freeze quite well. Wrap it twice with plastic wrap, place in a baggie and mark the date. Wrapped this way the pastry will keep frozen for up to 2 months.

INGREDIENTS

2 pounds flour

2 pounds butter

2 1/2 teaspoons salt

1 cup water

1 cup heavy cream

Additional flour for rolling

Start by making crème anglaise (refer to recipe earlier in this chapter), but add 1 cup of heavy cream before you put into an ice cream machine.

COFFEE ICE CREAM

Add 1/2 cup ground coffee beans to the milk before you make the crème anglaise, then pass through a fine strainer. Once this is done, place into the ice cream machine and spin until ice cream is formed.

FOR CARAMEL ICE CREAM

Cook the sugar and water over high heat until it begins to caramelize. Remove from the heat and add the lemon juice. Then add 1/2 of the ice cream base to the caramel, and once it is mixed well return it to the vanilla ice cream base, mixing well. Pass through a strainer, chill, then place in the ice cream maker and spin.

PISTACHIO ICE CREAM

Add the liquors and pistachios to the ice cream base. Place into the ice cream maker and spin.

CRÈME ANGLAISE

7 egg yolks

2 cups milk

8 ounces sugar

1/2 vanilla bean

1 cup heavy cream

1/2 teaspoon salt

FOR CARAMEL ICE CREAM

1 cup granulated sugar

1/8 cup cold water

1 teaspoon lemon juice

PISTACHIO ICE CREAM

2/3 cup shelled pistachios

1 1/2 teaspoons Kirsch

1 1/2 teaspoons amaretto

1/2 teaspoon salt

ROASTED BANANA ICE CREAM

A very interesting ice cream flavor you won't find numbered among the 31.

TO MAKE ROASTED BANANA ICE CREAM

Preheat the oven to 350°. Using a small sharp knife make 6 holes in each of the 3 unpeeled bananas and place them on a small baking sheet. Roast for 10 minutes until black and split. Let cool then peel and coarsely chop. In a medium non-reactive saucepan stir together the milk, cream and sugar. Add the roasted bananas and simmer over moderate heat for about 8 minutes.

In a large bowl, whisk eggs yolks to break them up. Whisk in half of the hot milk and cream, then whisk the mixture into the saucepan to blend. Cook over moderate heat stirring constantly with a wooden spoon until the custard thickens and reaches 185° (about 4 minutes). Do not boil. Remove from the heat, stir in the other bananas along with the rum.

In a blender, puree the custard in 2 batches and transfer to a large stainless steel bowl. Let cool, then cover and refrigerate for at least 2 hours or overnight. (Alternatively set the bowl in a larger bowl of ice and chill 45 minutes, stirring occasionally.

Working in two batches, transfer the custard to an ice cream maker and freeze according to manufacturers instructions. The ice cream will keep for up to 5 days in airtight container.

INGREDIENTS

4 large ripe bananas,
3 un-peeled and 1 peeled and coarsely chopped

2 cups milk

2 cups heavy cream

1 cup sugar

8 egg yolks

1 tablespoon rum

1/2 teaspoon salt

HAZELNUT MERINGUE CAKE

This cake takes two days to prepare; one day for the meringues to thoroughly dry and the next day to assemble. This dessert is at its heavenly best the second day, when all of the flavors have had time to settle. To me, the agreeable combination of crunch, chocolate and cream makes this comfort food.

FOR THE MERINGUE

Preheat oven to 225°. Trace out 4, 8" circles on sheetpans lined with parchment paper.

Whip the egg whites until they are very stiff. Halfway through whipping, add a pinch of salt. When the egg whites are stiff, turn the mixer down on low speed and slowly add the sugar. (Do not over-whip or the sugar will melt the whipped whites.)

FOR THE MERINGUE

1 cup egg whites, room temperature

Pinch of salt

2 cups granulated sugar

3/4 cup finely chopped hazelnuts

Fold in the chopped hazelnuts. Place the meringue in a pastry bag with no tip and pipe into the 4, 8" circles, starting with a coil that ends at the center.

Bake the meringues for 3 hours. The meringues will begin to take on a light tan color. Turn off the oven and allow the meringues to continue drying out for at least another 6 hours.

THE NEXT DAY

Remove the meringues from the oven. They should be very dry and easily removable from the sheetpan. Be careful or the meringues will break if they are dropped or roughly handled. Place in an airtight container if you won't be using within the next few hours.

FOR THE CHOCOLATE BUTTERCREAM

Place the egg whites in a bowl and put over a pan of simmering water. Whip the whites until they become frothy. Add the sugar and continue to whip until the sugar melts into the whipped whites. Remove from the heat and add the cocoa. Mix well. Add the butter, incorporating well. Set aside to cool and thickens slightly. When the buttercream has cooled and thickened, stir it and put equal amounts on 2 of the 3 meringue discs.

FOR THE CREAM

Place the vanilla and water in a pan. Add the gelatin and warm on the stove until the gelatin has melted. Remove from the heat and reserve. Whip the heavy cream with the powdered sugar. When the cream is almost stiff, add the vanilla/gelatin mixture. Continue until all is stiffly whipped.

ASSEMBLY

Place one buttercream covered meringue on a flat cake plate. Evenly spread 1/4 of the whipped cream on top of the chocolate. Repeat this process one more time by placing the next meringue on top of the other and covering it with more whipped cream. Then place the unadorned meringue on top. Cover the top and sides of the cake with the remaining whipped cream. Sprinkle shaved chocolate all over the cake and refrigerate for at last 8 hours.

To serve this meringue cake at its best, remove it from the refrigerator 30 minutes prior to serving.

FOR THE CHOCOLATE BUTTERCREAM

3 egg whites, room temperature

1/2 cup granulated sugar

3 tablespoons cocoa

3 ounces bittersweet chocolate, melted

3/4 pound unsalted butter, room temperature

FOR THE WHIPPED CREAM

2 packages plain Knox gelatin

2 tablespoons vanilla

1 tablespoon water

3 cups cream

1/3 cup powdered sugar

COCONUT-LESS GERMAN CHOCOLATE CAKE

This is my birthday cake. It's the only cake I've eaten on my birthday for as long as I can remember birthdays. I love German chocolate cake, just not the coconut (thanks, Mom).

FOR THE ICING
Place all of the ingredients in heavy gauge pot and cook over a medium heat stirring constantly, until the mixture begins to thicken. Remove from the heat and cool to room temperature.

CHOCOLATE SOUR CREAM CAKE
In a medium sized bowl mix the cocoa, water and coffee extract. Then cream the butter and the brown sugar. Beat the eggs and add vanilla until mixed, add the creamed butter and sugar to the egg mixture then add the sifted flour, baking soda and salt, mixing gently. Fold in the cocoa and water into this mixture.

Pour the cake mixture into 2, 10" round buttered and floured round cake pans and bake at 350° for 35-40 minutes. Once removed from the oven, allow the cake to cool completely. Invert onto a wire rack.

TO ASSEMBLE
Slice each round in half, into two layers each. Place a cake disc on a flat plate and cover with icing. Repeat the process until all of the cake layers are iced.

INGREDIENTS
2 cups evaporated milk

2 cups sugar

6 egg yolks

1 cup butter

2 teaspoons vanilla extract

2 cup chopped pecans

CHOCOLATE SOUR CREAM CAKE
2 ounces cocoa

1 1/2 cups very hot water

1 teaspoon coffee extract

8 ounces butter

1 1/2 teaspoons vanilla extract

9 1/2 ounces cake flour

1 teaspoon baking powder

1/2 teaspoon salt

DIVINITY

Yes, this is that old fashioned treat – white, whipped 'clouds' of sugar with nuts. Please note: you have to whip air into the mixture with a spoon (not a whip). The trouble is, you have to avoid overwhipping or it will become too dry. (Who said cooking was easy.)

Blend the sugar, syrup, water and salt in a non-reactive saucepan and cook over medium-high heat until the syrup reaches 240° on a candy thermometer. Remove from heat. Beat the egg whites until stiff. Add about 1/3 of the syrup mixture to the egg whites. Return the remaining syrup to the heat and continue to cook until the syrup reaches 270°F on the candy thermometer. Blend this with the sugared egg whites in the mixing bowl, then add the vanilla. Beat until stiff. The mixture should be very dry and fluffy. Fold in the chopped pecans. Place tablespoon dollops of the divinity (with an oiled spoon) onto a parchment lined backing sheet. Set aside for 15 minutes to fully dry. When set, store in an airtight container.

INGREDIENTS
2 1/2 cups granulated sugar

1/2 cup white corn syrup

1/2 cup cold water

pinch of salt

2 egg whites

1 teaspoon vanilla

1 cup chopped pecans

WHITE CHOCOLATE RASPBERRY TART

My friend and Pastry Chef, Chan Loi, of the Bedford Village Inn created this white chocolate sensation. She was and still is the best pastry chef I have ever known.

TO MAKE THE TART DOUGH

Preheat oven to 375°. Blend the walnuts, butter, sugar, egg, orange zest and flour in a mixer on low speed until thoroughly combined. Press the dough into the tart pan, Bake shell approximately 20 minutes or until a light golden brown. Cool completely.

TO MAKE THE FILLING

Place the raspberries evenly in a single layer in the tart shell. Heat the cream and butter in a saucepan and stir in the white chocolate. Remove from the heat and stir until smooth. Pour over the berries, tilting to level the filling if necessary.

TO FINISH THE TART

Drizzle with the dark chocolate and chill well before cutting. Heat a knife in a container of very hot water. Wipe the knife dry and while still warm, start cutting. Repeat this process until you have cut the desired number of servings. Be sure to wet the knife and dry it before each cut to ensure a nice, clean line.

FOR THE TART DOUGH

3 3/4 cups walnuts chopped fine

4 ounces (1 stick) butter at room temperature

3 tablespoons sugar

1 egg

1 teaspoon orange zest

1 1/2 cups all-purpose flour

FOR THE FILLING

3 – 4 pints raspberries

1 pound white chocolate, chopped fine

2/3 cup heavy cream

3 tablespoons butter

1 ounce semi sweet chocolate, melted

This is a mouth puckering, wonderfully rich citrus dessert. Amazingly, once the tart shell is baked, the filling is made completely on the stovetop. Raspberries and lemon pair well together with this dessert.

TO MAKE THE TART SHELL

Roll out the sweet pie dough to 1/16" thick. Line a 10" tart ring with the pie dough, wrap with plastic and refrigerate tart shell for 1 hour. Preheat oven to 350°. Line the prepared tart shell with aluminum foil and place 2 cups of dried beans or rice inside. Bake for 30-35 minutes or until lightly brown. Remove from the oven and remove the beans and foil. Reserve the shell.

TO MAKE THE LEMON FILLING

Whisk the eggs, egg yolks, lemon juice, lemon zest and sugar together in a heat-proof bowl. Place this bowl over a pot of simmering water. Whip the mixture over the simmering water until it thickens to a ribbon stage. Remove from the heat, add the butter a little at a time and whisk until incorporated. Press this mixture through a fine strainer with the back of a large spoon or spatula. Pour the filling into the prepared pie shell. Refrigerate for at least 4 hours.

TO MAKE THE RASPBERRY PULP

Place all of the ingredients in a saucepan and cook until syrupy. Pass through a fine strainer scraping firmly with the back of a metal spoon. The pulp will be very thick.

ASSEMBLY

This tart can be served two ways. To serve individual slices, run a knife under hot water, quickly wipe it dry and cut the tart in half. Run the knife under the water again and wipe the knife well. Make a second cut so you now have four equal slices. Repeat this 2 more times until you have 8 pieces. (Warming the knife will give a clean cut every time. If you don't heat the knife, curd will cling to the knife and the edges won't be 'clean'.) Lightly sprinkle each slice with the sugar and glaze with a propane torch or under a red hot broiler for a few minutes until it melts and turns brown. Place a slice of lemon tart on a plate and top it with a spoonful of the raspberry pulp. Garnish with a few fresh raspberries and fresh mint leaves. Sprinkle with confectioner's sugar and serve immediately.

MISE EN PLACE

1 pound sweet pastry dough (Pâte Sablis)

1 recipe Lemon Curd (recipe follows)

1 cup Raspberry Pulp (recipe follows)

8 ounces sugar

FOR THE LEMON CURD

4 whole eggs

4 egg yolks

1 1/3 cup fresh lemon juice

Zest of 6 lemons

1 cup granulated sugar

1 pound unsalted butter, cut into small pieces

FOR THE RASPBERRY PULP

3 pints raspberries

1/2 cup granulated sugar

Juice of 1 lemon

FOR THE GARNISH

Fresh raspberries

Fresh mint leaves

confectioner's sugar

To serve as a whole tart, sprinkle the tart lightly with the sugar and glaze under the broiler or with a propane torch for a few minutes. Remove the tart from the pan and place on a cake plate. Spread about 1 cup of the raspberry pulp thinly over the curd. Line the outer rim of the tart with a circle of fresh raspberries and tuck some mint slices in and around the rim. Sprinkle with confectioner's sugar and serve.

MAYHAW JELLY

Makes 1 pint

This is a very unusual jelly, which also happens to be my favorite jelly. I grew up in Louisiana, where mayhaw berries were a part of Southern culture. Every spring my Mom would make this jelly. The aroma of it being prepared rekindles fond childhood memories. As it cooks, mayhew jelly produces a wonderful, aromatic smell.

Wash the berries thoroughly, removing stems and spoiled berries. Do not remove the green berries as they contain pectin that makes the jelly congeal.

JUICING OUT
Place the washed berries in a large container or pot with enough water to cover. Bring to a boil and cook until juices turn bright pink. Line a large colander with a clean cup towel and pour the liquid and berries into the towel being careful not to mash the berries. Be sure to have colander in a large enough pot to avoid overflow.
Repeat as many times as necessary until all the berries are gone.

COOKING JUICES
The best jelly is made in small quantities. Cook 3 cups of juice to 2 cups of sugar at a time. Cook to 220° and pour immediately into clean jelly glasses. When cool, seal with paraffin.

FREEZING JUICES
The juice can be frozen successfully for an indefinite period of time.

INGREDIENTS

Mayhaw berries

sugar

My version of a traditional napoleon layered with wonton skins instead of puff pastry, fresh fruit, pastry cream, and caramel sauce. A huge seller at Citizen.

TO MAKE THE FRIED WONTON

Separate the wonton skins. Preheat a fryer to 450° or place 4 cups of vegetable oil into a heavy gauge pot and heat to 350°. Fry a few wonton skins at a time until they are crisp and brown. Remove from the oil and allow to dry on a dry towel or paper towel. Reserve. Wontons can be made 2 days in advance if kept in an air tight container.

TO MAKE PASTRY CREAM

Prepare cream as directed in recipe. You can flavor the pastry cream with anything you choose such as grand marnier, rum, kirsch, almonds, etc.

TO MAKE CARAMEL SAUCE

Mix the sugar and the water together. Place them in a heavy gauge pot and bring to a boil. Continue to boil until the sugar begins to caramelize. Once the caramel has reached a nutty brown color remove pot from heat. Carefully add cream to caramel, going slowly so that the caramel doesn't erupt and cause a burn. Whisk in the butter and keep warm.

ASSEMBLY

Lay a fried wonton skin on the middle of a plate. Spoon 1-2 tablespoons pastry cream onto the wonton skin. Gently spread the pastry cream over the surface of the wonton. Place the fruit on top of the pastry cream. Repeat the process. Then add the final fried wonton on top of the second layer, sprinkle generously with powdered sugar and place a sprig of mint on top with a few raspberries. Spoon the warm caramel sauce around the wonton napoleon.

INGREDIENTS

12 fried wonton skins

1 cup Pastry Cream (see recipe in this chapter)

2 cups assorted berries such as raspberries, blackberries, strawberries or blueberries

1/2 cup caramel sauce

powdered sugar

FOR THE CARAMEL SAUCE

(Makes 2 cups)

1 pound sugar

3/4 cup water

1/2 tsp fresh lemon juice

1/2 cup heavy cream

3 oz. unsalted butter

TECHNIQUES

SECTIONING CITRUS

Cut off the top (stem end) and bottom of the fruit. Resting the fruit on one of its cut ends, take a paring knife and cutting downward with a slight sawing motion, cut between the pulp and the white pith. Hold the pared fruit in one hand and with the other cut the pulp out of each of the sections slicing between the membranes. After the fruit has been sectioned, squeeze the membranes over the fruit, swathing them with juice. Cover and chill.

TO CUT LEAVES INTO A CHIFFONADE

Chiffonade literally means "little rags." In my case, it means anything leafy cut into a fine julienne or finely shredded. To make a chiffonade of basil, simply stack no more than 6 leaves one on top of the other and roll up tightly widthwise (from top to bottom). Don't roll it the other way because if the leaves are cut against the vein, they will turn black fairly quickly. Hold your basil "cigarette" tightly and with a very sharp knife, make quick work of slicing the basil into very fine strips. Somehow, it always seems appropriate to "fluff" a chiffonade after you cut it.

Other items that the technique of chiffonade can apply to:
Sorrel, lettuce, spinach and Napa cabbage - in other words anything flimsy enough to take the roll.

TO MAKE PARSLEY JUICE

1 large bunch of flat parsley
1/3 cup grapeseed oil
1/4 cup chopped ice
salt and pepper to taste

Blanch the parsley for 20 seconds. Shock in ice water. Drain and pat dry. Place the parsley, grapeseed oil and chopped ice in a blender. Blend thoroughly, about 30 seconds. Season with salt and pepper and reserve.

SALMON STEAKS

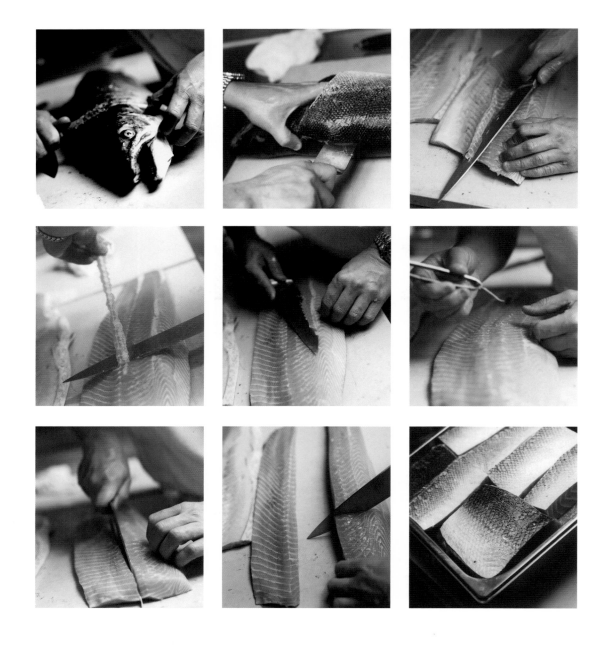

TOMATO CONCASSÉ
or how to peel, seed, core and chop a tomato

Tomato Concassé (kon kas say) is tomatoes that have been peeled, seeded and uniformly chopped. This technique is indispensable in a restaurant kitchen and I use it throughout a workday. Make only what you need, because once treated in this manner, the tomatoes will begin to lose flavor, texture and color.

Remove the stem scar from the tomatoes. Mark the bottom of the tomato with a shallow "X" that cuts just through the skin. Place the tomatoes in boiling water for 30 seconds or until the tomato skin begins to peel away where you made your cut. Immediately shock the tomatoes in ice water to stop the cooking. When the tomatoes are cooled sufficiently (about 1 minute), peel the skin from the tomato with a knife. Lay the tomato on its side and cut the flesh away while rolling the tomato. If you've done this correctly, you will have a long piece of tomato flesh. It's okay if the flesh is in a couple of pieces; you are about to chop it up into smaller pieces anyway. Blot up any excess juice on your cutting board with a paper towel and lay the flesh in front of you. Cut into the desired shape. For use in this book the cut is what I call a concassé, or an evenly cut small dice; do this unless directed otherwise.

THE MERCURY
Plano, Texas

THE MERCURY GRILL
Dallas, Texas

CITIZEN
Dallas, Texas

SPECIAL THANKS

Special Thanks to Debra McCarty, Todd Blakenshipp, their administrative staff and Tracy Parsinen.

DIRECTOR OF OPERATIONS
George Majadlani

CHEF DE CUISINE
Tim Bevins   Norman Grimm   Yutaka Yamato   Keith Hicks

SOUS CHEF
Colleen O'Hare   Delfino Lujano   Hector Cabrera

GENERAL MANAGERS
Fernan Perea   Downing Riley   Ari Levy   Mario Cutulo

None of this could have been possible with out my Restaurant Life Culinary team,
waitstaff, hostesses, bartenders, and service staff.
Thank you for all your dedication and hard work. It is greatly appreciated.

SUR LA TABLE 1-800-243-9852 • **SELECT FISH** 8080 N. Central #1390 Dallas, TX 75206 214-207-5354 • **KAZYS GOURMET** 9256 Markville Dr. Dallas, TX 75243 972-235-4831 • **THE MAYHEW TREE** 105 Mitcham Circle Tiger, GA 30576 800-262-9429 • **ALLEN BROTHERS MEATS** 3737 South Halsted St. Chicago, IL 60609 773-890-5100 • **UNITED SEAFOOD** 4008 Commerce St. Ste 200 Dallas, TX 75226 214-887-8009 **AMERICAN PRODUCE** 4721 Simton Rd. Dallas, TX 75380 972-385-5800 • **PREFERRED MEATS** • **CENTRAL MARKET** • **J.B. PRINCE** • 29 West 38th St. NY, NY 10018 212-302-8611 • **BRIDGE KITCHENWEAR** 214 East 52nd St. NY,NY 10022 212-688-4220 **PETROSSIAN CAVIAR** • 182 West 58th St. NY, NY 10022 212-245-0303 • **GOURMET INC.** 2869 Towerview Road Herndon, VA 20171 703-708-0000 • **JONES LOBSTER FISHERMAN** • P.O. Box 313 Hampton, New Hampshire 03843 603-926-3311 • **LANDLOCK** P.O. Box 841414 Dallas, TX 75284 972-241-7500 • **DAHLGREN DUCK** 2554 Tarpley Rd. Carrolton, TX 75006 • **LUCY ZIMMERMAN** 972-221-5257

Thanks to Judy Walgren, John May, and Clint Smith
for their help in creating this cookbook.

INDEX

Grilled Asparagus and Caper Bacon Dressing, 156

Grilled Colorado Lamb Chop with Roquefort Flan
and Cumin Scented Lamb Jus, 125

Grilled Foie Gras on a Rhubarb Tart with White
Pepper Fruit Glaze, 146

Grilled Quail in an Herbed Popover with Applewood Bacon
and Chanterelle Braise, 68

Grilled Quail with Spaetzle / Black-Eyed pea Salad, 78

Grilled Rare Tenderloin with Chilled Sweet Vermicelli, Spicy
Cucumbers and Soy/Mirin Sauce, 130

Grilled Scallop with Kumquat Fennel Glaze
and Black Truffle Oil, 92

Grilled Swordfish with ginger/orange crusted oyster and
chicory salad, 103

Grilled Yellow fin Tuna with Green Onion Noodle Cake, 95

Halibut Wrapped in Bacon, 83

Hazelnut Meringue Cake, 174

Heirloom Tomato Salad with Sherry Basil Vinaigrette, 52

Hidden Poached Egg on Toasted Sourdough and Mustard Oil, 47

hors d'Oeuvres,
Chilled Spring Rolls, 36
Eggplant caviar with Country Bread, 37
Pecorino and Fresh Mint Canapés, 33
Quenelle of Fresh Ricotta with Shrimp and Basil Mint Pesto
on Grilled Sourdough Bruschetta, 32
Ricotta and Anchovy Canapés, 33
Shrimp in Kataifi with Purple Relish, 35

ice cream
ice cream, 173
Caramel, 173
Coffee, 173
Pastichio, 173
Roasted Banana, 174

Imperial Rolls, 44

Jalapeño Cheese Grits, 160

Java-Cured Beef in a Parmesan Crisp
with an Almost Caesar Salad, 40

Kalamata Bread Salad, 51

Kataifi Crusted Shrimp with Green Olive Tapenade
and Citron Pepper, 96

Kobe Beef Tataki with seared Foie Gras, 149

lamb,
Grilled Colorado Chop with Roquefort Flan and Cumin

White Chocolate Raspberry, 177

Tempura Crisped Shrimp with Asian Pesto, Roasted Roma Tomatoes and Grilled Eggplant, 107

Tenderloin of Beef with Braised Short Ribs, Béarnaise Sauce, Mousseline Potatoes and Baby Arugula Salad, 132